A Reason To Live

Every Day & Every Way

Chris Wilkins

Dedication

I dedicate this work to every person who has ever felt lost, or who may still feel lost, and that may or may not be you at this very moment. I have a little story I like to tell about being lost which neatly sums up my beliefs about being, well, lost.

My wife and I like to ride around in my Jeep with the top down and the doors off. On bright sunny days she usually says, "Hey buddy! Let's go get lost in the Jeep," and then she hugs me real hard so I will say, "Yes," which I always do. During one of these "getting lost" jaunts as we were meandering up and down a steep, rutted and twisting mountain road in north Georgia, we stopped to ask a fairly ancient gentlemen walking along the side of the road where we were, just for posterity's sake (and to see if he needed a ride).

In his best southernese and smiling kindly he asked, "Well, are you young 'uns lost?"

Grinning, I replied, "Oh no sir! We still have gas in the tank!"

Contents

Chapter One

The Stuff of Life

How does an idea for a book about reasons to live, let alone one reason to live, take shape? How did the genesis come to pass? For me, writing this book was personal. Very personal and very intense. An apt description of the writing experience for me can be found in the quote from sportswriter Wellesley "Red" Smith (often incorrectly attributed to Hemingway) as to the arduousness of writing, "You simply sit down at the typewriter, open your veins, and bleed."

This was certainly the case for me, and when I finished the writing of this book I felt an immense sense of accomplishment while simultaneously experiencing a deep, cellular exhaustion. I had been bled dry, and I needed to rest my mind. Interestingly, books are never really completed, and my experience has taught me that there is always another possible revision or addition... But, back to business. The "Why" of this book.

Perhaps, you have downloaded this book because you too, like me, have thought about reasons to live, breathe and just be. I think this may actually be a universal activity which happens for all people, and I am sure it takes place with varying degrees of intensity. Some may simply think about "life" as they are walking to school or riding the bus, while others sit for days, weeks and months meditating about their existence and how it correlates with the rest of the Universe's plan. Reading this book more than likely is (and I do wonder about things like this) a personal event for you. Personal and maybe... private, and that is perfectly okay - as it should be.

You see, it's personal for all of us. Life, after all, is a very personal thing, and our relationship with ourselves is the most important relationship we will ever have with anyone (other than God for some).

I have met a great number of people who are very aware of their "aliveness." With each breath taken they feel an overwhelming sense of responsibility that their lives cannot, and should not, go to waste. They are acutely aware in their sentient condition that... they exist. What they are not sure of is whether that matters, or more specifically, if they matter. I think this consideration enters the distant, and not so distant, corners of consciousness for many of our planetary denizens, we humans.

"Do I matter?" is a question every sentient being asks at some point. However, after much reflection induced by circumstance that threatened to shorten my life, I believe that is the wrong question. I think a much more appropriate question is "What matters?" or perhaps, "What people, places and things matter?" You know. The stuff of life. The stuff that matters.

Some time ago I sat in the hospital musing about my not-so-great circumstances at that moment, and I started making a list of all the people, places and things in my life that matter. I was surprised at how many there were and was equally surprised at the variety and differences between them. There was, indeed, a full spectrum of people, places and things that mattered, and consequently, were reasons to get up in the morning and carry on. In many instances, it was more than just carrying on that mattered, and instead of simply surviving, there are a good number of "people, places and things" that make me truly exert myself with zeal so I can thrive.

Upon closer examination, I could see that each was, and is, a thread woven into the tapestry of my life, and I believe they provide evidence of a life well lived. A colorful tapestry in the making, and I am its main protagonist. Of course, we are all weaving a tapestry on the loom of life that is as individual as each and every one of us, just as it should be.

The day before the creation of the list, I had been transported by ambulance from a small hospital in the mountains of north Georgia to one of the large medical complexes in Atlanta. These medical complexes are not only hospitals. They are enormous, complex and multifaceted, and in their largess, they are more like small cities comprised of multiple hospitals, each with their own specialty, accompanied by all of the facilities that support them and their areas of expertise. The logic of having all of these interdependent facilities close together and within proximity of each other does not escape me. It makes perfectly good sense, but they are also overwhelming. Feeling "lost" in their enormity was a feeling that I became quite accustomed to, and I am sure there are many, many hospital veterans who know exactly what I mean.

But I digress. Let me take you back to the small hospital in the mountains... My wife had driven me there because my calf had swollen to twice its normal size, was red and warm to the touch. Prior to our arrival, with Dr. Google in her hand, she had quickly deduced that I was probably suffering from a DVT, standing for Deep Vein Thrombosis. This is a blood clot, or clots, in the calf muscle that are very, very dangerous as the clots can let go and travel through the bloodstream and cause either heart attacks or brain aneurisms. As we were preparing to leave the house, which was 18 miles away from the hospital and down a winding dirt and gravel road in the proverbial boonies, I began to feel fatigued. I just felt a sense of overwhelming tiredness, so much so that even breathing became a nuisance. I wasn't out of breath. It was just a conscious effort to breath continuously and calmly.

Normally, it is a 45 minute trip to the hospital. With my partner Mario Andretti driving, we got there in 20. As we were admitted to the small (it has eight in-patient rooms), but efficient, hospital, they took all of my vitals and lo and behold, my pulse was holding steady at around 32 beats per minute and at one point it dropped to 28 bpm. I was still very much conscious and holding a normal conversation but definitely fatiguing right away when I tried to walk. They rolled in the crash cart and asked me to stay seated and not get up anymore. The doctors looked anxiously at each other and spoke in hushed tones in the corridor. I heard one say, "Well, here we go," and for the first time, anxiety began to steadily creep into my thinking. *I was becoming nervous.*

There were a flurry of tests which, incidentally, is very tiring as well. X-rays. Urine. Blood. My body was checked form head to toe. A very long and slow hour passed by, my wife sitting next to me holding my hand and rubbing my back, and the doctor walked in. The head of the hospital on that particular day. The very first thing she said was, "We do not have the equipment to treat you here. An ambulance is waiting outside to transfer you to Atlanta." It was shocking to hear. Alarming!

What do you mean you don't have the "equipment?"

She went on to explain that I had a saddle pulmonary embolism. Five emboli in each lung to be exact. She also further explained that I could have a heart attack at any moment and instructed me to take it easy, stay calm and all would be well.

Okay. Yeah, sure.

Please note how I devote an entire separate line to, "Okay. Yeah, sure." It certainly deserves it. Even in my nervous, and now scared, state, I was still a wiseass. That's just me. By the way, who would have ever thought to combine "wise" with "ass," but it really does make sense (he thought wryly).

Needless to say, and evidenced by these very words, we made it to Atlanta and they were already prepared for my arrival. Someone had called ahead and greased the skids. The young man taking care of me during the ambulance ride was a veteran of the Afghanistan war, an army medic, and his skill set was impeccable (said the man with absolutely no medical training). He explained that everything he was doing with me he had learned in the service. I felt a surge of pride as we rode, and I thanked him for his service. We chatted the entire way, and as he wheeled me into the ER he looked into my eyes and said, "I saw a lot of situations when I was in Afghanistan, and I can tell you this, you're going to be fine sir." I was thankful for the reassurance. Actually, I was more than thankful. I needed to hear those words, "...you are going to be fine sir." Mentally, I was deteriorating. Fear does that.

We went straight into "prep" for surgery: IVs, drugs, gowns and breezy backsides. The plan was to run a catheter into my leg and remove the offending clot from my leg and then, with the use of Heparin and other clot dissolving drugs, rid my body of the very dangerous and satanically positioned clots in my lungs. It did not go well.

Unfortunately, the clot in my leg extended from my groin to my ankle and the doctors were fairly impressed by the sheer size of it. One of them let out a low, soft and long whistle, "That's a big one... " As they tried to remove the clot, they broke two catheters in my leg. After the failed second attempt, they decided to rely solely on the drugs. When I was in recovery, the doctors asked me how I felt, and I honestly felt so much better! *In fact, I felt great!*

The surgeon explained that they had been able to remove about 50% of the clot, and the drugs would quickly dissolve many of the smaller clots so I would see improvement right away. He also noted that it was remarkable that I was still alive, and as we sat and cracked morbid jokes about escaping the grim reaper, he asked if I worked out, which I do. I work out five days a week. Mostly weights but quite a bit of cardio mixed in as well. After thirty years, it has become part of my lifestyle, and it is part of who I am.

He looked me dead in the eye and said, "Your working out saved your life. Make sure you keep doing it." I haven't missed a week since. Not that I needed much more incentive – but still...

I decided at that point I was not done living, and so, I continue to weave my tapestry and the following pages contain some of my reasons to live with an accompanying scene from my life's tapestry.

My fervent hope is that you find inspiration and motivation in these pages, and I wish you joy and peace.

Chapter Two

Love

It is here, amidst the loom of love, that our lives can generously and magnificently be portrayed if we take the time to connect and weave together all of the caring, nurturing and loving threads connecting us to people, places and things.
— Author

Ethereal. Overwhelming. Exhausting. Motivating. Exquisitely delicious and equally painful. These are the words that come to mind when I think about the oft-used word "love." Sometimes I think we use it so often in passing that we forget the import and hefty weight that the word actually conveys. It is not to be trifled with. Not to be toyed with. After all, people die for love. They move mountains for love. They build, create, suffer, endure... All for the sake of, and in the name of, love. Sometimes for just the promise, just for a fleeting taste, of this most abundant and awkwardly elusive elixir of life. The sweet, sweet enchantment of love. In my book, it is the number one reason to live.

I struggle to define love which is different than describing it; and conversely, it is easy to state what it is not. For me, sometimes clarity can be found when I very purposefully set out to define an idea, concept or theory by pinpointing what it is not. This allows me to build some defining boundaries - a box, if you will, where I can then narrow my thinking about a particular thing.

Following this train of thought, what love is not, my mind went straight to the concepts of hate, darkness and evil. More specifically, a darkness of spirit, mind and body where greed, excess and depravity are the greatest character achievements and life is individual-centric and selfishness is the guiding principal for one's action or inaction.

Within this narrow backdrop for what love is not, perhaps love is simply to do what is right for the highest good of all concerned on a societal scale, and at the individual level, love in such a manner as to nurture, share and create an uplifting relationship with self and others. And perhaps, perhaps, there will be that one, the one special person, that feels the same about you. The soul mate.

So, with this "thing" called love, I opine and believe that it is without doubt the greatest motivator that exists, and I daresay that when we harness the power of love, we latch on to the unending and everlasting threads of the universe as they weave their tapestries through time and space. It is here, amidst the loom of love, that our lives can generously and magnificently be portrayed if we take the time to connect and weave together all of the caring, nurturing and loving threads connecting us to people, places and things. To portray them through love... with ourselves and those we care about.

I once heard someone say, I can't quite remember who or where, that "we should strive to live in the light." As I ponder the gravity of the statement, I can't help but equate it to "we should strive to live in love," because to me they, light and love, are one and same, and if my reason for getting up in the morning is to imbue the tapestry of my life and the lives of others with love, boundless and free, then I do believe that is a wonderful, fulfilling and glorious reason to live.

However, I think there is more to love. My own experiences have taught me, shown me over time, that love is not always tender and soft, or as my kids will jokingly say, "all unicorns and rainbows." Sometimes, the exercise of love's passion is thorny and leathery tough and to endure it, one must possess grit and faith. Let me explain.

My wife and I were recently having a quiet discussion about love over a wonderfully aromatic and velvety glass of wine, and the topic turned to "falling in and out of love." One might think that because of the topic selection (which came to light organically through conversation) that we were having a problem with our relationship; however, nothing could be further from the truth, and actually, it is the polar opposite. Our relationship, which we have carefully and conscientiously nurtured over the years, allows us the freedom and safety to talk about anything. From falling in and out of love to wondering what in the world we ate to create the zeppelin filling amount of gas that is now propelling us around the house (a new fuel source I believe – should bottle and sell it). Absolutely nothing is out of bounds. That too is love.

I believe it is a fairly universal reality for most people that you can't be in euphoric love all the time, and in fact, there are times when the euphoria and wanderlust in one's eye for the other person has dimmed considerably. I chuckle here because I can recall with great clarity the time my ex-wife threw her high heel shoe at me from across the room. It cut through the air as if propelled by some magical and powerful force, and then there was a loud crack as the stiletto of the high heeled weaponry impaled itself in the wooden closet door. This happened when we were still relatively happy at the beginning of our relationship, and in spite of that, the shoe flew. I am just thankful that her aim was so poor.

Of course, it is normal to have disagreements and even pretty intense arguments (stiletto heel throwing is not normal by the way), but perhaps it is unexpected to one who has just fallen dramatically in love and suddenly senses or feels that the overwhelmingly charged electricity of love is waning. It can be, as most of us have experienced, alarming. The question surfaces in the mind like a monster rising from the deep subconscious, "Am I falling out of love?" as perspiration beads on our brow and our chest constricts with each breath. This question, of course, "Are we, am I, falling out of love?" sets in motion entire rivers of anxiety as hurricanes of fear lash at the shores of our every thought. "Is this the end of the road for us?" Woe is me! "I had such high hopes this time..."

Karla, my wise shaman companion, noted that love was like the ocean, vast and beautiful and subject to the ebb and flow of the tides as the world spins and the moon exerts her gravity upon her friend, the Earth. Relationships, like the ocean, have numerous pressures and forces affecting them and these create an inevitable ebb and flow in the feelings of closeness and intimacy, and similarly, this ebb and flow also affects the energy levels and bandwidth available between people in a relationship. Babies are born. Jobs are difficult and time consuming. Cars break down. Partners travel. Bills must be paid and the toilet needs plunge. Sometimes, the euphoric lust and romantic depth of new love must take a back seat to the principles of "doing what must be done" and "burning the midnight oil" so the house can be heated, babies can be fed and the bills can get paid. Of course, that too is love if one chooses to see it for what it is. Committed trust in the relationship.

As we neared the end of the glass of luscious wine, we both agreed as our relationship has blossomed and deepened over time, it is the sure knowledge that the ebb and flow of love's amorous passions is natural, and sure as the tides come and go, so it is also with those feelings. Of course, having that degree of faith and trust in the relationship, the certainty in the relationship, is key to being patient with the process. Patience with the relationship and patience with your lover and friend that all is well can only exist when there is trust.

As I savored the last sip of honey dew vine water from Willamette (rhymes with dammit) Valley, my definition for love became clearer, as now I could see it was our ability to talk about literally anything that allowed my wife and I to feel safe and secure, and this in turn allowed us to trust in the relationship and in each other. Consequently, it was this trust that allowed us to be patient with the ebb and flow and the ins and outs of everyday life as it affected the movement of the partnership day in and day out. And so it is, that our relationship has ebbed and flowed many, many times over the years, and I can say with great certainty that it will continue to do so.

This same truth is applied to many other relationships that are loving in nature, but of course not in the carnal sense. But, nonetheless, on various levels, these same principles work with all relationships.

Chapter Three

Create

Caged creativity is a travesty of the soul.
— Author

So, almost 53 years on the planet and just recently I came face to face with the demons and angels of mortality. I think mortality, in the sense that we think of it, could be an angel or a demon depending on our particular paradigm and experiences leading up to our appointed hour at death's gate. Is the Grim Reaper not also the Great Liberator, and the idea of a permanent ending can come as a great disappointment, or she can also come as a great release... from pain, from fear, from cancer, from loneliness...? And therein lies one of the paradoxes of death and the perceptions we have of it.

As I lay in the hospital bed, which was absolutely too small for my six foot five inch frame, I took stock of my life and the enormous good fortunes that I have had, and do have, in my life. However, where my mind took me was surprising, and I have to say, I was awed by the destination that I arrived at in regard to what is important and what is not important to me.

My mind kept turning to three things over and over and over. Broken record like (a simile which is a complete anachronism for people my age), I found myself thinking of Karla, my companion, friend and wife, my children (and now as I rewrite and edit – my grandchildren) and my writing. Hovering in the extended periphery of my consciousness was my extended family and friends whom I care about deeply, but what was interesting were the feelings that I had towards my writing. Toward my creations. It was almost as if they are... a part of me. An extension of my own persona. I do not think it is so much creating as it is carving off a slice of myself or perhaps "my self" to be served up on the page to satisfy the reader's appetite.

In fact, upon my very deliberate escape from the hospital, one of the first things I told Karla, best friend and confidant, was we needed to get my book published right away because I had had an epiphany, and if ever I were to perish and leave this world, it was very important that my writing, my written offspring, were given a chance to live out in the open world of ideas, passions and creations. I needed to give them the opportunity to exist by their own merit and worth. They needed to be set free. You see, in my view, caged creativity is a travesty of the soul, and I can't bear the thought of my written offspring being jailed for all eternity.

It was not a spontaneous understanding that occurred upon looking in the mirror. There was no eureka moment that allowed me to blossom into full understanding at the enormity of the revelation that creating is one of the greatest focal points in my life and is, in fact, one of the single greatest motivators in my life. It gets my motor going. It gets me out of bed. It gets me psyched up to see what the day holds in store, and I love everything about it.

No. It was days and days of, accidentally (as in lying in a hospital bed for days on end) reflecting on my thoughts that ultimately brought me to the conclusion it is the act of creating something, not just with the written word, but with any medium that allows me to express myself in a way that brings me a deep sense of satisfaction, truly at the psychic and cellular levels. This could be the building of our dream house, which my wife and I do together, working with my photography, working on the writing or searching for the very specific and exact words needed to complete a line of poetry or prose. All these creations are equally painful for me, and I do not suffer the joy of writing until the birthing has been completed, and then, ahhh then, there is a wonderful feeling of satisfaction and bliss as you stare down into the eyes of the newborn poem or paragraph.

I have a ritual, perhaps a process, I have fallen into when I am writing. I take my central idea or theme and I write the word or phrase in the middle of my five foot wide whiteboard which has both a front and back. I carefully make a perfect circle around the word, and then I brainstorm. It is a process that happens in starts and fits, and it is incredibly fun as it merges both a spontaneous stream of thought and the more cerebral process of connecting ideas, themes, anecdotes and concepts. As ideas come, I begin to make word clusters around the central theme, and the process builds and builds as one word or idea leads to the next until the entire whiteboard is completely full and the central idea, the circled word or phrase in the middle of the board, has been "fleshed out" so to speak.

I do not rush this process as taking an idea and moving it through its evolution is not easy for me. In fact, it can be quite painful both for my typing-so-slowly arthritic fingers and glasses-wearing head-aching temples as I become frustrated at my ineptitude in regard to stringing ideas together to create clarity. Sometimes, my thinking is a chaotic cacophony of ideas cascading and intermingling with each other generating an organic wordsmithing mush with absolutely no direction, and I am very much envious of people who seem to be able to push out entire concepts fully formed in an orderly, focused and distilled product. Bastards!

Once the board is full, then it is time to organize all of the "thinking," and it is this organization that leads to clarity which in turn become sentences which become paragraphs which become ideas made flesh. This is, of course, the goal: to give our ideas substance, the life giving blood, skin and bones necessary to walk, run and play in the world of the reader's mind that they may converse and share.

And it is for this reason, the incredibly deep sense of satisfaction that we all universally feel upon completing something unique and different as each one of us, that I believe the act of creation is one of the most compelling, beautiful, difficult and satisfying reasons to live.

Create something today and feel the joy. Feel the satisfaction and feel the life coursing through your veins that are yours and yours alone.

Chapter Four

Freedom

Freedom, our foundational principle imbued with the ideal that you are the Captain of your own body, mind and soul and you shall decide where your ship will navigate - not a government and not another human.

— Author

Freedom. Magical, transformational, liberating freedom. The highest application of our intellect, ideals and effort to reach for and become our highest and most successful selves, and perhaps, too, the ability to exercise our own choices in an effort to maximize and further our own ideas of what we each consider a meaningful and successful life. Too complicated? Well, let's try this: "I want to make my own decisions in, and for, my own life." Simple enough right?

This ability to choose for ourselves, though, has had an incredibly and unimaginably costly price, and the payment was made with the national treasure of our citizenry's blood, sacrifice and ultimately, lives. We enjoy freedom that was paid for by others, and this ability to use, enjoy and live within the framework of a free society is truly a golden opportunity and truly a blessed way to live life. It is without precedent in history, and this is without a doubt one of the greatest and best times to live in all of mankind's history thus far as noted by Harvard professor Steven Pinker, in his book *Enlightenment Now*. Given that we can live and fully realize our greatest selves, I consider freedom a really fortuitous and wonderful reason to live. Especially, at this point in our unfolding history.

However, like most things in life, I find that "freedom" exists on a spectrum. You can be more "free" or less "free" depending on the culture and society or environment you live in, and, by the way, I find it interesting that the society you live in is actually an extension of the environment in its totality.

An interesting example that exists in today's day and age would be related to the current US political environment and the newly arisen global "Cancel Culture." In many regards, this greatly reduces our freedom of expression and choice. It's easy to argue this point with some well targeted questions: would you travel to Portland, Oregon, and visit downtown next week? If you were a Donald Trump supporter, would you wear your MAGA hat or Trump t-shirt in downtown Detroit? Are you pro or con in regard to Covid-19 vaccinations and boosters?

In most cases, you can be fairly certain that undertaking and exercising your freedom to choose will result in some aggressive behavior from other citizens and thus, put you at risk. So, just as earning freedom came with a hefty price tag, exercising your freedom can also come at a price - a price that can have significant mental and, in some cases, physical costs. So, it would appear that when we exercise freedom we also have to calculate the outcome and the risks associated with those choices. Freedom isn't free.

Benjamin Franklin, after having signed the US Constitution, was asked by a woman on the street what had they, referring to the Continental Congress, given us to which he replied, "A Republic, if you can keep it." As I reflect on the divisions in our society, I can't help but take note of the poignant choice of his words. Democracy and the freedoms inherently contained within it are not guaranteed, and interestingly, I see the continual creep of democracy's demise in many areas of our culture, both here at home in the USA and globally as well: *I am referring to intolerance.*

We are beset by legions of intolerant warriors who want to strip you of your freedoms and instill a new set of norms, values and codes for society. The irony is that they are doing this in the name of inclusion. Their mission is to exclude in order to include, and the inherent outcome of such a course is plain to see.

Cancel Culture warriors want you to only enjoy and participate in products, people and organizations that adhere to their narrow philosophy and viewpoint; if you dare to do something different, they actively try to damage you (or your organization) financially and reputationally. They blackmail you into agreeing with them not comprehending or caring that agreement based on coercion is not an honest sharing of an ideal, concept or philosophy. It is nothing more than blackmail.

Wokeism wants you to believe, and they have a mission to change all education in our country to adhere to their belief, that all white people are racist, even if they don't know it. They push an agenda that promotes Critical Race Theory which astonishingly boils all issues down to skin color. Condoleezza Rice had it right when she stated that we can teach our children about the atrocities of racism in our history without making little white girls feel bad about themselves and the color of their skin.

Transgenderism has made it illegal in some places to call a biological man a man if they "identify" as a woman, and further, you must adhere to calling them by their preferred pronouns, and if you don't you could lose your job. Ironic that in their quest to be included and accepted by society, they have become completely intolerant of other points of view and beliefs. A Christian, Jew, or Muslim who believes in only the binary man and woman is now an enemy of the "enlightened" and must be castigated should they refuse to use the preferred, regardless of the very evident biology, pronoun. A psychologist who believes that the person is suffering from body dysmorphia and has a form of delusion called Transphobia is now ostracized by entire communities for fear of losing their license and business practice. Again, acquiescence by force and fear is not agreement.

Now, it is important to see both sides of every coin lest you do not understand the currency of how social exchanges take place. The marketplace of ideas and movements always has two sides (and many times more than two) to the coinage they use for their transactions. The rise of these movements is a direct byproduct of the oppression that various, *and many*, groups within our society have endured. That is a fact, so these movements are based in grievances that are very real and very tangible.

Similar, if not identical, to the Taliban, we have had in our history, and continue to have today, many religious organizations that are intolerant to the extent of complete exclusion of anyone who does not completely agree with their tenets and Godly appointed and derived scripture. I for one am suspicious of any God given decree that says gay people, as just one example, are going to burn in Hell and that everything about them is inherently evil. A person's sexuality is suddenly the determining factor as to whether or not they can enjoy their version of salvation? I believe God, the maker of all that is and beyond, is much more loving and inclusive than the narrow minded pastor who preached such painful ideas and then prays for and wonders why the suicide rate is so high in the gay and transgender population. All the while, this particular congregation only allows men to be the conduit to God while women are not viable candidates for direct conversation with, or interpretation of, God's word.

Yes. We can see how religion, even though much good has come from these organizations, has also been the conduit for much harm and exclusion. All in the name of God.

As I sit here and speculate, while writing and eating pancakes in my favorite IHOP, I can only wonder how many wars have been fought, how many men and women have died and how many orphans grew up without parents – all in the name of God.

I would venture to guess that the actual reality is that two opposing viewpoints, in their arrogance, believe they were, and are, right about everything, and with intolerance as their mighty shield, set about with violence, both economically and militarily, to prove their point. When violence becomes the chosen method you use to prove your point, your point is no longer provable or defensible.

Oh, there are many, many other forms of intolerance that have emerged and joined in the fracas with all of the old intolerant viewpoints that infect our society today, but now there are so many varied and violent infections in our country's body that one wonders if it will be able to recover? When everyone thinks they are right, who is wrong? As everyone promotes their own agendas and beliefs and vociferously trample the rights of others, what has become of freedom?

In the United States of America, freedoms are articulated and framed in our Constitution and they have limits - limits designed to assist the citizenry in working, living, thriving and interacting together as a society with common goals but perhaps not values. We recognize these freedoms as "rights," and they are varied and many, and usually, those rights are well thought out. And, thank goodness for limits!

You don't have the freedom to hurt someone else. You don't have the right to drive as fast as you like endangering everyone else on the highway, and you don't have a right to dump your garbage into everyone's collective water supply, right? Rights, or freedoms if you will, are measured against the good of the individual as they affect and pertain to the good of the community at the local, state, national and global levels.

Freedom, it would seem, is a highly regulated set of behavioral ideals, thus our thousands upon thousands of laws, designed to allow for maximum human creative opportunity and growth for the citizen while simultaneously insisting that the same liberties for all of the members in a society are equally protected. To put it succinctly, as you chase your dream and work to fulfill it, please don't trample on mine.

Freedom is our foundational principle imbued with the ideal that you are the captain of your own body, mind and soul and you shall decide where the ship of your person will navigate - not a government and not another human. You and you alone are the captain of your ship and this can only happen when you are free.

So, again, freedom is an incredible ideal and reason worth living for, and I ask you, what have you done with your freedom today?

Chapter Five

Chance

It does not matter whether you think your future is already scripted or if the page hasn't been written yet - we do not know the form that the future will take.

— Author

Even though we human beings have many, many powers, so to speak, clairvoyance is not one of them. Ahhh, yes. There are some who would argue that this is not the case; however, if anything, my experience has taught me that we never know what is waiting right around the corner. We never, ever, truly know what lies in store for us, and this simple fact has been brought to my attention time and time again by our little friend and trickster, life.

That is not to say we shouldn't plan, chart our courses and follow our dreams from the present into the future; it simply means that as we do so, we can absolutely count on the unexpected, the unplanned, the unpredictable and the unexplained as over and over chance plays her hand, and we are handed one opportunity after another to become who we are.

The chance encounter with one of our high school classmates that say they have been thinking about us, and there was this new job that just opened up where they work and would we be interested?

The chance find as we are putting on our winter coat and headed to the store for baby formula but don't have a dime to our name and then as we put our hands into the pockets we find a twenty that we had lost and forgotten about last winter.

The chance discovery that we love the world of plant biology more than we could ever have imagined while working towards our goal of becoming a veterinarian, and so, a lifelong goal suddenly takes a sharp turn in another direction.

The chance introduction by a friend to their brother who has come over to help jump start your car because the battery is now on its very, very last leg and has become an electrical cripple not capable of even lighting a flashlight much less start a car. Quite suddenly, and unexpectedly, by the time the car has started so has your social life as you have a date with the very car smart friend's brother, and your stomach is a veritable butterfly storm that you haven't felt in years.

I think it is important to note that chance, opportunity if you will, does not always get laid on our doorstep as a bouquet of flowers. Sometimes it will be the bag of not-so-sweet-smelling pooh the prankster neighbor's kid has left on our door for one perceived slight or another, just as was the case with the dead car battery. But, one thing is for sure, having chance show up in your life can be a wonderful and unexpected event. Who knows? Sometimes change can change your life.

My dog Spencer is a wonderful example of chance, and I probably should have named him Chance; however, when he came to live with me and be my friend, he already had his name, Spencer. A furry snicker doodle bar if there ever was one with his brown and white fluffy coat, he used to belong to my daughter, and we had specifically found the little bundle for her because she was uncontrollably homesick in her first year of school away from home. She was very lonely and very unhappy away from home, but, and there is the proverbial "but," alas, she was not allowed to have pets in her apartment mostly due to roommates and his insatiable appetite for affection. He is a lover through and through. So back to our home he came, very much still a rowdy, energetic and needy puppy.

Eleven years later, Spencer is the bringer of joy, lion at the front door, guardian of his flock (and I do think I am included in that), and he is neurosis in the flesh. Without a doubt, my day in and day out companion, and even at this very moment whilst I write these words, he is curled up at my feet in front of the desk. If I dare to venture upstairs into the kitchen, he will make the journey with me. Sometimes, there are treats involved where the kitchen is concerned, and this is very well known to him. Come to think of it, now that I am taking a close look at my 23 pound friend who should be 18 pounds, I may need to put him on a diet... Mea culpa Spencer. Mea culpa.

The universe is full of endless possibilities and the wildly delicious and scary truth of it is that we do not know what the future holds in store for us. It does not matter whether you think your future is already scripted or if the page hasn't been written yet. We do not know the form the future will take. Just as Edison did not know that the light bulb would take 2,774 tries, and Walt Disney did not know he would almost goes bankrupt numerous times. You just never know. Will this be the good news, the bad news, the make or break of who you are at this moment in time? Only by living and moving forward on the time continuum will we know what chance has in store.

Chapter Six

Cause

When likeminded people get together to achieve a common goal, the impossible becomes possible.
— Author

To make a difference. To apply ourselves in such a way that something we believe in, that is important to us, that is in alignment with our values and thoughts, has a better chance of coming to fruition with our efforts, energy and intellect behind it.

This is to have a cause; although, it is not enough to have a cause. There also has to be the commitment to apply ourselves to it, to devote our time to it, in such a manner that we are propelling it along towards culmination.

Just because you are part of a cause doesn't automatically mean you are also part of its success or failure. This in large part is dictated by the degree to which you become vested in the cause in-so-far as your daily life, daily energy and daily thoughts are concerned.

First comes the thought, then comes the word and then comes the deed, and indeed, a cause is one of the best reasons I know to get out of bed in the morning and make the difference that so needs to be made.

The Humane Society volunteer who wakes up every Saturday and makes their way to the shelter where 152 dogs and cats eagerly await their arrival because they are sadly, forlornly, starved of love and attention and they await the loving ministrations from gentle and caring hands.

The veteran who works every day to ensure that veterans returning from Afghanistan and Iraq receive the care they so desperately need as their minds deteriorate under the onslaught of sleep deprivation and PTSD tremors which won't allow them to reintegrate back into the society they protected and which, in some cases, now shuns them.

The environmental activist who has given hundreds, and perhaps thousands, of their living and breathing hours to help ensure the safety of sea turtles along the 1,600 miles of Florida's shoreline. A shoreline that wages a constant war with numerous interests including those of real estate developers, cities, counties, the Army Corps of Engineers and a tourism industry that is probably the largest in the continental United States. All of these entities are among the predatory consumers, sometimes unwittingly, of the sandy beach where the sea turtles nest. The enormous task of protecting the nests and baby sea turtles seems daunting, unrealistic and, frankly, impossible. Yet, somehow, when enough like minded people get together and work towards a common goal, the impossible becomes possible.

When my stepson Sean was a youngster, somewhere in the neighborhood of 10 to 11 years old, he was in love with everything that was related to, around and in the water. In this case, the specific body of water was the Atlantic Ocean which was adjacent to where we lived in south Florida. At that time we owned a scuba diving shop, and for a young boy of ten years old a scuba shop is pretty much the equivalent of heaven. A heady mix of adventure, fun and exciting gear and lots and lots of friends and customers who shared their love of the sea with him.

He learned to scuba dive when he was 10 years old and was literally quite amazing with his skills. For practice, he and I would bundle up all of our gear and throw it over the side of the boat and watch it sink to 50 or 60 feet beneath the waves, and then we would dive in and swim to the bottom sporting only our swimming trunks. Upon reaching our gear in the blue green depths, we would methodically and carefully don all of our gear, and after crosschecking our gauges and gear, we would give each other the "OK" signal and begin our dive.

For the fresh eyes of a 10 year old, the underwater world is nothing short of magical, and of course, the reverse is true as well. Sean saw firsthand what pollution can do to a reef and to an entire ecosystem. He was very, very offended by this. He would frequently ask me why I was letting pollution happen and what was I going to do to stop it. Deep inside of me I felt the rumblings of adult responsibility for the future of our children, and these were also the tender and first beginnings of Sean's understanding about the negative impacts of human society and civilization upon the natural world around us. Just as the reef's beauty opened his eyes with wonder, the ever-present pollution cast a shadow on his beliefs about human activities and motives.

Our little dive shop became one of the first donors for the newly formed Reef Rescue of Palm Beach, and by virtue of this, Sean was introduced to an entire legion of people dedicated to the preservation and protection of everything Sean loved in and around the sea. One of these was a student with the University of Florida and she needed volunteers to help with a big study the university was commissioning to study sea turtle nests, eggs and hatchlings. What an opportunity for a 10 year old boy! A way to give back! Needless to say, Sean was elated, but here is where the story becomes more interesting for me as a father.

As the summer weeks unfolded into luxuriant long hot days, they asked if Sean would meet the team at 6 am on the beach to count nests, eggs and hatchlings. Yes. You read that correctly. 6 am. To be at the beach at 6 am we needed to get up at 4:30 am, get ourselves dressed, fed and everything else that needs to be done when one wakes up and heads to work. Then from 6 am to 9ish or 10 am, they worked. Yes. They worked.

Remarkably, Sean said, "Yes." He would work with them and leave each morning at 5:30 am (meaning Karla or I would as well), and he would do something about the pollution problems he was witness to. In that moment I fully understood how the power of a cause could transform a person's psyche and behavior. I began to recognize how important it is having something to care about. Caring and doing matter to the person's inner core and character. When you care about something, you become a better person.

The rewards for caring I think may be immeasurable, and I say this while I think about Sean running up to the car in full on 10 year old excitement mode telling us about all of the turtles they had counted, seen and helped that morning. Hundreds and hundreds of turtles and he was there with them, among them, guided and coached by another caring adult, and all the while he felt good about everything he was helping with – and life overall was better.

Herein lies the magic of the cause: When likeminded people get together to achieve a common goal, they will all experience growth and nurture in the process. The impossible becomes possible, and to become a part of that, to become part of a genesis of a good cause, well, that is a great reason to get up every morning – even if it is 4:30 am.

Chapter Seven

The Seasons

Step out, outside, into the world where the senses push outward to understand our environment and our elemental nature.

— Author

To feel the heartbeat of the seasons as they give way to the years, while they in turn build the millennia, has always been a powerful allure for my eyelids to flutter open in the wee hours when the night gathered dew still clings to life on the needle, petal and leaf. My morning puffy eyelids in turn seem able to convince the comfortable rest of me to sally forth into the promise of a new day, albeit the chill in the air will cause the body to forfeit the warmth of the home and hearth.

Aahhh... To step out, outside, into the world where the senses push outward to understand our environment, our elemental nature and then inform the mind and the soul of how and where we are... this, this is to live fully in the present. One breath, one day, one season at a time. There is no yesterday, and there is no tomorrow. There is just now and that, my friends, is a very liberating and exhilarating way to experience each day.

For me, I find that to actually honor the passage of time, to relax into to it and not fill it with obligations and things that artificially seem to be of utmost import but really are not, this is to be fully engaged with the seasons. Ironically, I also find I am most productive when I approach the expenditure of my precious time in this manner. Simply put: I get much more done when my mind is fully engaged in the present, in the moment, than when it is consumed by events that have already happened and those other ethereal events that have yet to occur.

The irony does not escape me that the present can be so adversely affected by events, things and actions that haven't yet occurred and may, at the end of the day, never occur. And yet, they preoccupy our minds, and it is the occupation of the mind that pushes out the present like a foreign invader on sovereign land. Our minds are hijacked and occupied by a future which can in no way have the same miraculous beauty and impact as the moment we are currently experiencing *in the present*.

I also find it interesting to note that my affinity for one season over another has changed with my age. When I was younger and my blood ran quick like the sap in the trees on a long and hot July day, I was without a doubt in love with summer and everything summer brought with her. This would have been the summer of 1981. By any stretch, a very good year regardless of the very high interest rates at the time.

I was out of school, and every day was suddenly a holiday to be experienced to the fullest with my ever-growing list of abilities, freedoms and friends. This particular summer, we'd spend each waking moment planning to get our very brown and lithe bodies to the beach to get burnt by the blazing rays, play any number of sports on the beach and then as we rode home, plan all of the necessary logistics of getting to the beach the following day. Mostly it was frisbee, and we ran at full speed, launching ourselves into the air with youthful elastic legs, in flight for just a few precious seconds, while our outstretched arms and hands snatched the flying disc from lofty heights before we were engulfed with a thunderous crash in the blue green and never ending waves. It was a full time endeavour and no mean feat to accomplish.

As August arrived and I finally turned my thoughts to the new school year that was coming, I remember sitting in the living room one Saturday morning when the phone rang, and, by the way, this was a rotary dial phone with a line attached to a phone jack (aka plug for you young folks) in the wall, and as my friends told me about the day's logistical hoops that we would jump through to get to our beloved beach, I heard myself saying, "Guys, not today. I think I'm beached out..." Can you believe it? I was actually tired of the beach. Incredible but understandable, just as it is understandable that my favorite seasons should change with my age. Things come and go in our lives and seasons are some of our first teachers in this regard.

Now, at 58, I find myself in the autumn of my years, and yes, you guessed it, my favorite season now is fall. I know... I know... Trite, and yet honest, if you must know the truth. Fall seems to amplify my reflective nature at this point in my life and my thinking. As the leaves turn bright orange, red and yellow and the spectrum swings from the aliveness of summer to the preparations in fall for winter, it mirrors, perhaps, the same preparations I have begun to undertake as I, we, prepare for our lives as retirees and grandparents.

I used to be afraid of Winters. So cold and so barren they seemed, but now, I am not afraid, as I trust that when the winter of my life arrives, I am fairly certain my new favorite season will be Winter with its promise of new life and new beginnings in the Spring. The older I get the more forward thinking I become while completely enjoying the exact place and time that I am in.

The present, after all, is where we actually exist.

Chapter Eight

Beauty

Cherubic in nature, as all children's faces are to me, I am in complete awe of the mystery and complexity of life that is now fully realized in front of my eyes.

— Author

We are surrounded by beauty, and it abounds in our lives if we just stop to recognize it. I am reminded of the old adage, so trite and yet, so true: to stop and smell the roses...

I recall in my mind those things that awaken within me an appreciation, and provide the ample fodder for gratitude, and as I take stock in them, inventory them, I see that they are really quite simple and one of the themes that continually emerges in my life is that of simple beauty.

I had a chemistry teacher once tell me that there is nothing complex in the world; there are simply many simple things strung together, one after the other and the key is to remember and/or find a mechanism to remember the sequencing and order of these simple, but many and myriad, tasks or things. And, so it is with beauty.

As I glance upward at the skyscraper, I fully realize the engineering magnificence of the edifice; however, it is the simple straight lines juxtaposed against the blue sky and reflective and glossy surface of the marble facade that illuminate my mind with the fact that it is beautiful.

I study the child's face, cherubic in nature, as all children's faces are to me, and I am in complete awe of the mystery and complexity of life that is now fully realized in front of my eyes; yet, it is the simplicity of two eyes, a nose, a mouth and wispy tendrils of newborn hair that have happened billions of times before, that allow me to see the utterly magical and simple beauty of the sleeping child. Breathe in and breathe out dear child that we might all live and breathe with you.

Longingly, I keep my visage fixed on the horizon where the setting sun is getting ready to drive his chariot into the burning waters of the far away western sea and the colors of the sky will transform themselves from their blue palette to that of orange, red, purple and pinks and for this, my senses delight; and yet it is simple. A color change. The circular orb of the life-giving sun will sink out of sight, and yet, there is more. There is just so much more of beauty than what the eye can behold, and oh... there it is. That particular shade of pink that only sunsets can create.

I was, and still am, and English teacher and a big proponent of Project and Problem Based Learning. I am a huge fan (all 250 pounds of me) of learning by doing, and there is an amazing amount of research to support that this is probably the best way to learn. After all, you don't learn to ride a bike by reading a book about riding a bike. You learn to ride a bike *by riding a bike*, and if you know how to ride a bike you know that is true. I still have yet to find one single solitary person that will admit they read a book about it first. Come to think of it, I don't think I have ever even seen a book about riding a bike, and, yes, you can go ahead and chuckle now. I'm chuckling right along with you.

I bring up my teacher past because one of the things I find most interesting about beauty is how it flowers and manifests amongst we humans. I have yet to find one student who did not possess a beauty in them as unique and wonderful and different as they were. I had so many students display and live beauty in so many ways; from the student helping to tutor another with patience and care, to students writing poetry so poignant and pure that I was completely stunned... and incredibly humbled to be their teacher. The poet, who was in eighth grade at the time, and I worked together to submit her poem to a national poetry magazine for high school students.

In another instance I had a student who was in a fairly violent gang not because they wanted to be, but because that was the life they knew and lived on a daily basis. For this story, let's call him Ese as that as how everyone referred to him. His real name was... Oh well... Ese will do for now. Both of his parents were in the gang as well, and how I came to know this is another story for another day, but if you are a teacher, you know how vital it is to get to know your students and the lives they lead.

One sunny and lovely Florida day, I saw a fight brewing as all of the students in the vicinity encircled the protagonists in this daily occurrence in the inner city. I waded into the melee and quickly discovered that a much larger student had a much smaller student cornered and sitting hunched on the concrete floor of the large outside courtyard, and in between them was Ese. "What's going on Ese?" I asked using a stern but calm voice, so I could begin to deescalate the situation. Very calmly, his eyes locked on the larger boys eyes and never wavering, he explained that the larger student wanted to fight the smaller student because he didn't like the way he was looking at him. Ese had explained that the student was too small to fight, and it was not a fair fight. But, there Ese stood with his two bunched up fists raised in front of him, and defiantly he said, "But, Mr. Wilkins, I told him he can fight me instead."

Even in the most extreme circumstances, the inner core of our beauty can surface for all to see, just as the students surrounded our would-be pugilists, they could see the valor and courage of Ese protecting someone he thought was getting a raw deal. Not all street justice is right or moral, but as Dr. Martin Luther King noted, "Just because it's a law, doesn't make it moral." In this case, we all took the high road and no fights were to be had on that day and the encircling circus ring made of the student body, soon dissolved and went about the business of getting to class. Nothing to see here today except maybe the beauty of Ese's courage.

I am reminded of the adage "we see what we want to see..." and this I believe could be the case with beauty. We must be open to see the reflection of our beauty within to the beauty that we experience without. Very simply, be open to the beauty inside of you that you might experience the beauty all around you.

Chapter Nine

Sharing

*Just a simple transaction where both parties feel better about
the positive net result of their worlds and their experiences.*
— Author

Such a simple thing, but the enormous impact of sharing on the
psyche, with and upon the Soul, does not come close to conveying the
fulfillment we receive when we share. To share is not to divest oneself
of possessions or material goods; rather, it is instead to invest in one's
own greatness, goodliness and Godliness.

And then there is the actual concept of sharing with all that it
holds. What can be shared? I would argue that literally everything
can be shared, and the entire premise for sharing can be distilled down
to two universal questions: what does the recipient need and two,
what does the benefactor have in sufficient quantities that they can

part ways with the item (physical in nature and otherwise) without suffering? These are the two questions that will drive the sharing transaction, and yet, we can add one more layer to the equation.

What if the person doing the sharing does not have enough and by sharing they will suffer? It happens. Ask any parent. Ask any friend. Most people I know will absolutely share what they have if they are aware of someone else'e great need, and they will gladly endure suffering without the item or "thing" knowing that what they did was important to the other person and in fact, they helped someone who is now better off than they were.

Things you can share? Food. Money. Home. Transportation. Friendship. Ideas. Direction. And most importantly: time.

One area I consistently believe is critical to our youth today, as it was to yesterday's youth and will be for the youth of tomorrow as well, is the sharing of time and space with adults in an activity that is nurturing and promotes growth and wellbeing. Note that I didn't specifically say growth and wellbeing for the young people only, but instead I would posit that both parties, the young folks and the adults they are working and spending time with, benefit greatly from their time spent together.

I look back and think about all of the sports I was involved in, and equally important to my sports activities, were the high school newspaper, poetry club, drama club (where I was a carpenter because they needed a stage and I am pretty sure they did not want me up on the stage during the main event) and I am keenly aware of the impact these activities, and in particular the adults leading them, had on the man and person I have become today. The time they spent with me, and all of us, in these activities was far in excess to any financial compensation they received. Entire weekends, (which were not required for the adults, but they went and led and guided us anyway), were devoted to many of these activities, and they enriched our lives immeasurably.

As an adult I became very involved with the Boys and Girls Clubs, and when you walk into a fully functioning and active after-school program you can actually feel the gratitude when you walk in the doors. It is palpable, and the smiles on the children's faces and their engagement in their various projects, sets the tone for the each and every day. As I would move through the hallways greeting each student, one of my favorite things was sitting and chatting with the students. It is enjoyable getting to know them, and they are more than happy that someone is interested in their lives and what they have to say. It is very uplifting and empowering to be heard.

They would tell me all sorts of tales about their lives, but one common thread always came up over and over when I was sitting in a well-run and happy after school program. The vast majority of students said that the program was the highlight of their day and they "endured" regular school just so they could attend the afterschool program. This was particularly true for those students who were "at risk" students, a label that seems to know no boundaries and serves as a catchall phrase for those headed toward to becoming a dropout statistic.

There were several instances where I pressed a little harder for information as I was looking for a way to guide and help them, and many was the time when I heard, "Well, Mr. Wilkins, this is the only place where I can me and where someone actually listens to me."

So, the sharing of time, and perhaps the lending of an ear as well...

Of course, where sharing is concerned, there is also the salt, the milk and every single other item you can think of. Neither one is more important than the other, and it all boils down to what is needed by one and what can be freely given by another with no strings. No expectations. Just a simple transaction where both parties feel better about the positive net result of their worlds and their experiences.

Chapter Ten

Grandkids

I am very much aware of my responsibility to her life and my responsibility to the society where she will make her way someday.

— Author

Exactly two years ago, a redheaded cherub alighted into our lives on a cold and wintery day, and when I first gazed upon her, the ground beneath me shifted, the hospital corridor warmed and my heart grew two sizes in my chest. Instantly, I felt I knew the Grinch like no one else did. Sorry, Jim Carey, I have the inside track to the Grinch's deepest thoughts now. I along with every other grandparent on the planet.

I had no idea how much love resided within me until the first time she happily and quietly uttered the words, "PaPa," which has since morphed into, "Where's Papa?" These last words spoken by the round-eyed cherub wearing a complete look of wonder on her face and looking imploringly upward for answers to this and perhaps also, where are the chocolate chip cookies.

There truly is this special quality to spending time with and loving and nurturing your child's child. Just as when our children are born, adopted and absorbed into love's family quilt, I am simply astounded at the depths of feeling evoked by their presence; the very same is true for Grandchildren.

And yet, there is a difference. There is a keening of the senses where infants and small children are concerned as they are beheld by their elders, and there is also a significant increase in patience and wisdom that was not there when we were younger parents for our own children.

When my second granddaughter was born, amazingly, the same feelings of love, gratitude and humbleness happened all over again, and thus, again... but with a more measured cadence, it became clear that my heart, once again, was growing. The difference was this: now I understood something important. Something profound. A realization so penetrating, that I think about it every day and when I do, I realize God exists a plenty. It is this: my heart, your heart, nay... the heart of humanity can and will grow infinitely. Loving is not finite. It is infinite.

My two granddaughters are also a magnificent handful, and as all seasoned grandparents will tell you, the two happiest moments of a visit with the grandkids are seeing the headlights coming up the driveway as they arrive and then seeing the brake lights heading down the driveway as they leave. Grandchildren are synonymous with exhaustion, and there is a very good biological reason that children are born into a young person's arena. It is by shear willpower alone that

Karla and I are able to power through a weekend of babysitting or, and God please be merciful with us, a week of vacation sitting (again, God please be merciful). But here again, it is this infinite love that we feel for our children's children that has us offering our home time and again for these beautiful visits.

Exhaustion be damned! I would never give up an opportunity for even a second to see the cherubs in action as they speed across our oak wooden floors on plastic Harleys, skidding scarily close to the sleeping dogs in turn number two on the race track that runs through the kitchen, around the dining table, in between the two sofas and then back around the kitchen island. That would complete one lap. Twenty nine to go, and I am happy. So very, very happy to be The Papa.

Our children have already told us in no uncertain terms, "More are coming. Get ready!" as we all happily laugh at our good fortunes while we watch our family grow, and plan for futures that have just begun to unfold. Then while cooking is practiced with plastic Little Tykes kitchens and future homes are built with Legos, we turn our attention to their learning, to their families and to the very near future which appears to arrive gradually but actually does so suddenly.

Grandchildren, it would appear, are the conduit to our understanding that we truly are a community – a brotherhood and sisterhood, and if I may, a humanityhood, that can be united in love for one another such that we care for, do for and are in service for each other that we may all have successful and fulfilling lives.

Sitting here, watching my redheaded fiery tempered two-year-old friend, who trusts me completely and without question, I am very much aware of my responsibility to her life and my responsibility to the society where she will make her way someday.

Chapter Eleven

Nature

To commune with Nature is a balm to the mind and a tonic to the spirit.

— Author

As I write this, below me the Cartecay River, green, clear and beautiful, is following the route it has carved out of the mountain over the millenia as it twists and turns toward Carter's Lake. This is not a quiet event at this particular juncture, and the riverbed has pushed a good number of rocks upward, forcing the water to hiss and boil over the ancient and smooth rocks. The result is the perpetual sound of loud wind rising up from the river and blending in with the cacophony of bird calls that make the enormous pines, elms, locusts and oaks their home.

The sound lulls me into a zen-like trance, and I close my eyes to better hear the river's song as it provides the distinct and never-ending soundtrack to carry the bird's melodious calls. It feels... never ending for now, and I can feel the changes begin to take place in my body, my mind and, yes, I think my spirit too. This happens every time. All I need to do is wait for it. Just exercise the smooth and relaxed muscle of patience.

My pulse has slowed and is still slowing, and I take a moment to reflect on my thinking, and yes, I sense rather than know, it has slowed as well. My mind, usually a bundle of fast moving pictures and sounds, has sharpened. The greater my communion with the trees, the birds and the river, the more in focus my thinking becomes... and accompanying this focus is a serenity, a calm that seems to have started in my mind and now has reached my arms, legs, fingertips and, finally, top of my head. Consciously, I set down the psychological baggage I have been carrying around all day and, in some cases, all week.

After ten minutes or so, I seem to snap out of my reverie. I become aware that for a moment, even though brief, I was not thinking about anything in particular. Just being. Existing. Enjoying the mental respite the sound and view of the river affords me, and I smile. Oh, how I have longed for this moment all day...

One of the most exceptional ways to view nature is by SCUBA diving, and as you may already know SCUBA is an acronym standing for Self Contained Underwater Breathing Apparatus. Once you are underwater breathing (can you believe we actually have systems that allow us common folk to breathe underwater? Amazing!) your mind will have shut down two ever present and very bothersome things: the past and the future.

As you are immersed into a foreign and potentially hostile environment, since you cannot survive the watery depths without special gear to keep you alive, all of your senses will become razor sharp, and all of your attention will be completely focused in the present. Of course, that is very important as you will need to pay close heed to various instruments that will allow you to monitor your depth, your position relative to a compass, the amount of time that has passed since you submerged yourself into the beautiful big blue and most importantly, your air gauge. Oh yeah! That little thing that tells me if I am running out of air! I smile widely as I think about this because as a diver with over 2,000 dives and having taught many students how to dive, I have definitely run out of air. Suffice it to say it is not pleasant and adrenaline, just like on dry land, under the water is a like a swift kick in the ass. Especially when you know you have just done something relatively inept and stupid that never should have happened. Frankly, it was embarrassing and humbling.

But, I digress, I was describing (before I went down the instrument's rabbit hole) how being under the water is incredibly beautiful. If you can imagine floating, almost flying, through the water since you are weightless, across the top of a coral reef where hundreds of species of fish are interacting in their habitat with many of them so preoccupied with their daily chores they barely take notice of your presence. Many are the time when I would settle quietly down in the sand next to the reef, trying to keep myself very still, and would eventually become surrounded by entire schools of fish as they were attracted to the shiny bubbles of air exiting my regulator. Cleaner shrimp, arrow crabs and octopus have sat in my hand resting or exploring on occasion, and I have watched as male sea horses shepherded their babies to and fro in the undulating currents with their tails wrapped around a sea fan. These images, these memories, are etched in undying ink into the most vivid memory banks of my brain, and they are a treasure to recall today.

To commune with nature is a balm to the mind and a tonic to the spirit, and I seek it often. Rivers, lakes, mountains, beaches, seas, deserts and the list goes on and on and all of it can provide the respite we need and certainly afford us a wonderful reason to live. To be part of it, to belong to it and to recognize this allows us to be. Simply be... at peace.

Chapter Twelve

Planning

The mind is liberated to a certain extent by the realization of the safety net that a plan portends for the future.
— Author

I sat quietly in the chair. A comfortable chair that was simple, yet elegant with its white linen upholstery and smooth long rocking motion. This particular chair was carefully positioned by the large window in our feng shui living room giving the person sitting in the chair a glorious feeling of open fields and great lake vistas, all while sitting within the confines of our living room.

This particular chair had me thinking. Reviewing where I had been, where I was and, just as importantly, where I was going. It was a moment of taking stock and measuring it against the dreams I had dreamed and the goals I had set twenty, nay... thirty years ago.

Then, perhaps thirty minutes into the "stock taking," I realized I had been doing this same routine for perhaps three to four days. Every day at the end of the day I was coming to the chair and sitting down for a meditation of sorts and taking stock of where I was. I was unconscious of the event, but there was no doubt as to what was actually taking place. So, upon this realization, I had to ask myself, "Why am I doing this? What compels me to measure my current circumstances? What am I preparing for?"

The answer was surprising and actually comes easily to one my age. Our mortality confronts us, and we begin to recognize as the body ages and doing anything and everything becomes harder and more difficult by barely discernable degrees. We will not be able to work forever, and we need to prepare for our latter years. Yes. These days sitting in the chair were about getting ready for retirement. Oh my God! That is where I have landed, and I cannot believe this moment has arrived here and so soon...

Yet, the inner clock that drives our daily habits across the days, months and years cannot be denied. Time cannot be denied regardless of the amount of lotion you apply to your face and body. So, now that I am fully aware of what is afoot in my unconscious, I have decided to bring it forward into the realm of the conscious, and I have formalized our preparations and our intentions. It is very true I am fond of charts and graphs, and I think I may be having an affair with my whiteboard. It's a very colorful relationship. Reds. Blues. Blacks and, of course, greens.

It is absolutely crucial and critical that you have a plan for your future – retirement or other. Otherwise, you are like a ship without a rudder, aimlessly drifting from shore to shore, sea to sea at the mercy of wind and wave and never reaching any destination at all except those accidentally brought about by chance. Usually, these can just as likely be a rocky and reef ridden shoreline as they can be a safe harbor. Thus, the adage, "Stay the course." But, I think perhaps first: chart the course.

As I have been moving through this process of planning, there has also been a dramatic shift in my levels of anxiety, or worry if you will, where the financial future is concerned. Oh, I still wake up at night and think about scenarios where we run out of money, where we can't pay the bills and where inflation runs rampant and outstrips our ability to keep up; however, now that there is a plan in place there has been a dramatic decrease in these thoughts and moments. The mind is liberated to a certain extent by the realization of the safety net a plan portends for the future.

It is more powerful than drugs and alcohol, and it provides one with a realistic level of self-control. It is also a sure way to establish some, but not complete, of course, control over the events to come. Can catastrophe occur? Of course, and that is also addressed in the plan with, and by, the investment of insurance in all of its expensive and various forms.

However, I think it is worth mentioning here because having a plan for the future, regardless of the life period you are in, provides something akin to peace of mind and more specifically, hope.

I believe with all of my heart that it is important for every life to have hope. For every one of us to know the future holds something in store for us that is important, safe and beautiful.

Certainly, one of the things I work on several times each week is this plan. It is a worthy and loving reason to get up in the morning and work toward continuing to weave the tapestry for a successful plan.

Interestingly, the plan isn't just for me; my entire extended family is included in the plan and therefore, the amount of satisfaction and peace I feel is amplified exponentially by the fact this planning affects my spouse, children, grandchildren and other family and friends as well, and this is a wonderful reason to live.

Chapter Thirteen

Teach

To share, instruct, empower, model and/or lead someone to an understanding, realization, or catharsis.

— Author

My credentials are those of a teacher. I went to school to become a teacher, and it was my fervent desire to ignite in my students the fiery passions and desire for learning. A yearning for learning if you will.

I wrote an article once in which I stated something to the effect of, "Today's students will solve tomorrow's problems with technology that has not been invented." Let that sink in for just a moment. We are advancing so fast technologically that an engineering degree starts to become obsolete, or at the very least "outdated," by the time the student is a university junior. There are also competing technologies and platforms that are simultaneously emerging and they both require specialization for the people developing, implementing and managing them.

Yesterday, I broke down as I was pulling out of the Lowe's parking lot in the North Georgia Mountains. My car, a 2020 Jeep Gladiator (right now all the Jeep owners are mad at me for calling my Jeep a car...), just stopped dead in its tracks and all of the lights on the dashboard lit up. That is a chilling and frightening sight because we all know today's cars are full of computer boards, chips, relays and PCM motherboards that control everything in the vehicle, and I have heard some say they also control the weather, tides and intergalactic movement of the galaxies.

So, you can imagine my consternation when I saw, and felt, this happen. I was put in the very unusual circumstance of being completely vulnerable at that moment and not able to help myself, and that is a very uncomfortable and humbling feeling. Thank God I had my iPhone, so I could call for help! Born in 1964, I come from a generation that was well equipped to "work" (beat with hammer to fix the problem as it retreats in submission – tail between legs) on our own cars, homes and anything else that broke or needed fixin'. Well, that is simply no longer the case with most everything! So, there I sat. The vehicle would not go into neutral because the new cars won't allow you to move them lest you break something in the process. That means the vehicle was stuck in the middle of the road. We tried to jump the car as well, but to no avail, and later I was told the new cars actually have a fuse that will blow if you try to jump the car and the voltage fluctuates at all. Well, if you have jumped a car before, you know the voltage is all over the place when you do that because of the draw on the donating vehicle.

At the end of the day, Georgia Mountain Wreckers came to pick me up in all of my shame, and the young fella doing the driving was about my age. So, there we were, putting the Jeep up on the flatbed, our two bald heads reflecting the sun back out to the upper atmosphere, while we commiserated about the good ole' days when we could work on our own cars, and then we bitched a bit about how expensive it was to get the new cars worked on now that every damn thing was computerized, electronic and glitchy as hell. Then he very gladly took my credit card and swiped it on his new iPhone with a Square payment chip reader and my bitcoin left my bank and went straight into his. I shook his leathery calloused hand as he said, "Sir, it sure was good to meet ya Buddy!"

I thought to myself, *Yes, I'm sure it was.*

So, why did I share the story you might ask? Why I am talking about Jeep Gladiators and computer motherboards? Well, to say this: if you think it is complicated now, just wait. Specialization will become exponential in the coming decades, and the interconnected nature of everything will very much become the disconnected nature of everyone. It will be very important to continue to evolve our educational platforms and methodologies to also include the cultural, emotional and mental arenas along with our technological growth. Perhaps, this is where you can help us learn something today? Perhaps you can focus your genius about life, love and happiness and teach someone about that too.

Teaching from the academic arena in so far as science, engineering, medicine, to name just a few, is an approach to learning that is only one side of the coin. It is a cogent argument as it pertains to the academic subjects, and I refer to this teaching methodology as exterior based. All of the "action" takes place outside the student's emotional realm. How you "feel" about this or that or the other is not taken into account nor does it matter.

The other side to the learning coin is the interior side of the pupil, and to teach someone to really make an impact on someone in a meaningful way, perhaps life changing for them as well, is truly an honor and an incredibly humbling and worthy reason to live. To address interior learning we must become engaged in understanding the student, the person we are working with, and we want to know what they think, how they feel and we also want to discover where they want to go and what they wonder about too.

Perhaps the key is to work with both sides of the coin in order for the educational currency to fully be actualized and used to its fullest potential for the student. One only needs to read about the effects of our social media driven discourse to discover how our students and youngsters suffer socially and personally due to dishonest representations and distortions that social media advertently and inadvertently create on their platforms. Additionally, social media viewership is driven by algorithms that drive extremely questionable and toxic content to eyes and minds much too young and ill prepared to process it. Students of all ages need to be taught how to ingest, process and make sense of what content is worthy of their time, energy and consumption and which is not.

However, students are not just youngsters in the elementary, middle and high school; on the contrary, our learning journey is one of a lifetime, so when I say a worthy reason to live is to teach, I mean to share, instruct, empower, model and/or lead someone to an understanding, realization or catharsis or provide a new direction for their forward path - regardless of chronological age.

Teaching has many paths and teaching has many faces. One of them could be your face, and perhaps you have something of value to share with others. Something they could use at this very moment, and as you sit and read this, you probably already know who it is and what you would teach them.

Chapter Fourteen

Hope

Hope does not live in the past, nor is it part of the future.
Hope is something we do in the present.
— Author

Hope is not a strategy, but it is certainly a lens through which we can view the world and, in particular, to see the world as one full of potential in a positive and nurturing manner. It is perhaps a place in the distant or not so distant future where we can see and believe in outcomes that are in our favor and in the favor of those whom we care about.

According to the Merriam-Webster dictionary, the verb "hope" is "to cherish with desire, with anticipation, to want something to happen or be true; to desire with expectation of obtainment or fulfillment;

to expect with confidence." As a noun "hope" is described thus: "desire accompanied by expectation of or belief in fulfillment."

How appropriate that expectation and fulfillment are two of the key descriptors of hope. It strikes me that our ability to hope, to project and think about possible expected outcomes in the future is in direct correlation and proportion to our greatest fears and most cherished dreams.

As I sit and reflect on this idea, I can visualize the "hope spectrum" in which the intensity of the feelings and hopefulness is aligned with the significance of the items we are hoping for. Sure, we hope we will lose that very pesky pound on our diet this week, that the always late mail will arrive on time this week or the grocery store will finally carry the correct canned tomatoes this week (why oh why don't they carry San Marzanos?). And, we also hope for the stock market to continue to climb, for our children to stay healthy and safe and for world peace to finally work its slow and steady progress into all countries on planet Earth. As I write this, just this morning the news was showing pictures of the citizens of Ukraine, men, women and children, lying dead on the streets, their cities destroyed, refugees by the millions pouring into neighboring countries. Hope never seemed as important as it does now.

Thus, as we think of hope in our thoughts it would appear it is in everything and knows no boundaries. Hope is part of our everyday lives and thinking. It informs the future with our dreams and a vision of possible outcomes for today - in the present.

To recognize that hope lives in the present is a very powerful realization. Hope does not live in the past, nor is it part of the future. Hope is something we do in the present, and hope is something that is vital to having a positive and constructive outlook on life. It is about seeing and thinking about the future in a positive way with positive outcomes.

But, what if you do not have hope? What if you have forgotten how to hope? How to dream about the future that is better or more fulfilling than your current circumstance? *What if you have lost hope?*

What if you feel hope... less?

There are very few things in life I am certain of, but this is one of them: at any time, at any place and under any circumstance you have the ability to hope. You just need to remember how: Simply think it. Believe in your ability to think of better outcomes even if just for one split second. Simply decide to think, dream and wish for a better...

Next second. Next minute. Next hour.

Next peaceful thought.

Next great meal.

Next sunrise, sunset, rainbow or blue sky.

Next... whatever brings a smile to your face, and you know what that "whatever" is better than anyone.

I spent a great deal of time in the hospital in the year 2021. It was a difficult and wonderful year simultaneously as I faced what would become one of my more serious health scares. However, before I continue, I want to stop and provide some superstitious context to my thinking when I was a 57-year-old man. My father, a good, kind and smart man, died well before his time at the tender age of 57, and my grandfather, who at one point oversaw the construction of navy ships during World War II, also passed on to greener pastures at the age of, you guessed it, 57. When I went into the hospital to have my spine fused, the result of a sports career that went absolutely nowhere but I still trained as if I were invited to the Olympics, it was March 26, two days after I had become 57.

As they wheeled me into the operating room, the anesthesiologist had already worked his magic, and I vaguely recall thinking, *I hope this goes well. I hope I wake. I hope I see Karla again. I hope…*

Then all was black.

When I awoke, a twenty-day ordeal ensued where the doctors and I battled together against an unseen foe that could only be identified with the assistance of a petri dish. I had developed a massive infection that went up my back and down my leg. I could not walk. I could not eat. I was having trouble thinking, and maybe worst of all, I could not sleep. I never fully understood how sleep deprivation works, but now I completely understand that not sleeping attacks your will. Your emotional reserves become exhausted as you battle day after day with powerful drugs coursing through your body, and as you lay there running on fumes, you begin to lose sight of the light at the end of tunnel. *It is a very gradual erosion of hope.*

My brother and I have for the last 30 years grossly joked about how we just need to get past the age of 57, and that is when the superstition began in my mind that we were somehow destined to leave this world at 57 as our progenitors had. A foolish notion of course, but, all the same, the dark thought bounced around in my head quite a bit as I lay there in my new digs, the hospital room, and I morosely noted how I was very much still 57 and the clock was ticking.

To my dismay, they had to "go back in," and a second surgery was scheduled so they could "clean up." Oh my! "Clean up." Sounds dirty and messy doesn't it? When the surgeon, a veritable genius and one of my personal heroes, made his first incision during the second surgery he said there was so much infection that when he made his first incision the semi clear, frothy liquid shot up three feet into the air, and everyone in the operating room jumped back. In a very, very strange way, I was so proud. I try not do anything half-ass, and yes,

I am acutely aware there may be something wrong with me. I mean, three feet? That has to be a record of some sort...

Slowly, as the days and nights became one indistinguishable long, confusing moment, my fighter's instincts took over. The competitive athlete came out to play, and I decided through drug-induced fog-laden thinking that I wasn't going down without a fight, and I love a good competition. So, I dug deeper. I prayed harder. I spoke to my wife, my champion in this life, every chance I got, and *I renewed my stores of hope*. I hoped about everything. I made a point to think about every single thing I wanted to do and had yet to do, and step by step, literally with a walker in my white-knuckled hands, I made a wonderful and full comeback.

Today I am 58 and stronger and more vibrant and alive than I have been in decades; mostly, I am hopeful for a long and fruitful future full of love, family and peace.

There can be no doubt that having hope and being hope-full is a wonderful reason to live. When one can be hopeful about the future, the present becomes a much more beautiful place to be, and hope can also affect how you act and behave in the present. For example, your vision of the future, your hope for the future, may necessitate that in order to achieve it you will need to go to great lengths and effort to secure that outcome.

The athlete that wants to compete at a very high level will need discipline, courage, drive and grit in the present to achieve the hope they can be a champion. The doctor that wants to save lives will need an incredible amount of courage to endure and succeed toward achieving the level of education necessary to reach their goal.

And it all begins with hope.

Hope is an expectation and vision of the future that informs our present with the behaviors we will need to get there. So, keep hoping and expecting the best - it will surely come your way.

Chapter Fifteen

Art

It is not the art itself, but rather, the resulting effect that art has upon us that truly matters.

— Author

Compelling. Emotional. Moving. Still. Complex. Simple. Elegant. Messy. Universal and personal. This is art.

I once toured the Louvre in Paris. I went alone and spent the entire day there. I recall how emotionally and physically exhausted I was as the day came to a close. The evocation and sheer volume of the emotions elicited from the art in my mind were many, powerful and ran the entire gambit of the human emotional spectrum.

I sat on a wooden bench in one of the great halls directly in front of the *Mona Lisa*, and I exchanged a long thirty-minute stare with her. Her gaze never flinched. She finally outdid me and won the staring contest, and I looked away, flushed from the effort and blushing with embarrassment, and I don't know exactly why. She seemed to be looking through me, and I felt very exposed with her gaze directed at me. When I looked back, her smile was still gentle, her visage was still unfurrowed and I imagined I heard her say, "Everything will be fine young man. Just follow your dreams." How fanciful I was as a young man. I think I still might be.

I have visited a good number of galleries, and it amazes me how many different mediums an artist has at their disposal to illustrate their ideas. From painting to sculpture and beyond, artists express their thoughts, ideas, concepts and stories, and each piece evokes and awakens within us a feeling, emotion, understanding and, in some cases, recognition of our humanity. Perhaps, as we feel what the artist intended, we feel the closer connection to their world and perhaps the world at large.

One piece of art that had a significant impact on me was a flag my students made in my English class for speakers of other languages. The demographics of this class were a microcosm of Latin American and the Caribbean as I had students from Haiti, Guatemala, Mexico, El Salvador and Jamaica. It was, without a doubt, an honor and a highlight of my career to work with these students every day. As I reflect back, I think that perhaps I was the student.

One day, one of the students noted the stories we were reading really weren't that interesting. They were old and had nothing to do with today's world and more specifically, their world. In short, they weren't relevant. Well, I can tell you from my own experience as a thirteen year old, if it wasn't relevant I probably wasn't interested. That's just life...

I decided to try something different to get their attention (and their buy in) because I desperately wanted them to practice reading and writing every day. So, I found ten stories about immigrants who had come to America and the trials, tribulations and triumphs they had had. The idea was that we would read in groups thereby practicing our oral language practice, have a larger discussion about the authors and their experiences, and then journal about our own experiences as immigrants as well. I was in the very fortunate position of having been an immigrant to Costa Rica, so I had some common ground with these young adults but in reverse. The American had gone to Central America.

The strategy worked! They became completely engrossed in the project, so much so they began coming to my classroom before school began to find out what we would be reading and discussing in the upcoming class. They were reading and they were journaling about their newly discovered common ground with the authors of these stories. In one of the discussions, they mentioned that as a class they wanted to create something to commemorate their new understanding of what an immigrant can be and is. We debated mightily. We discussed fervently. We were respectful as each voice was heard. After a few days, the students had their answer, but the answer came after we visited a local museum where the curator took a special interest in them and spent the entire day with them. They were smitten with his professorial tweed jacket, intellectual air and round spectacles. Such a gringo but so cool!

They decided, not me, to make an American flag out of plaster because they all liked the reliefs in the museum (they thought they were so very cool) , and then they decided to make a plaster mask for each of their faces which they would embed in the flag to represent that they too were part of the melting pot in the USA. Another student, my new star writer, offered up the idea that under each of the "faces" they could write a sentence or two stating what it meant to them to be a new American. I was astounded. Speechless, which for me is quite foreign.

They finished the project. Their art hung on the wall in the principal's office for all to see, and my students, well, special doesn't even begin to describe how they felt, but I assure you, the art they created intersects with their lives as immigrants every single day.

It is not the art itself, but rather the resulting effect art has upon us, just as it did for the students, that truly matters and is why I think art is a wonderful reason to live. It helps us to recognize the value of each of us as we put that value into context with the rest of society; a context which informs how we live each day, each moment, and how we appreciate, or do not appreciate, the present.

Visit a gallery and drink in the magic of the artist's creations and let them awaken within you the emotions and realizations that make the world more beautiful, amazing and complete.

Chapter Sixteen

Challenge

The resulting stamina and tenacity, or grit, become a new facet in the individual's character and begin to transform their pattern of daily thinking.

— Author

It seems counterintuitive that an obstacle or challenge in life would be a reason to live; however, I believe it to be true. After all, a life of ease with no hardships, no ups and downs and only ignorant bliss would cease to be the exciting, excruciatingly delicious, and worthy of our greatest efforts, existence. *Indeed, it is in our abilities and efforts to overcome our greatest and significant challenges that we become our greatest and significant selves.*

To go around, below, above and through the obstacle standing in between you and your version of success is perhaps the greatest of all teachers in life. And as we see time and again in our world, the greatest of accomplishments, in most cases, are preceded by the greatest drives, pushes and efforts. This holds true whether the accomplishment is on an individual, community or societal scale.

The process of engaging a challenge and seeing it through to its conclusion is unique in that it leaves the participant forever changed; growth cannot be undone, and the knowledge that if one tries hard enough, long enough and smart enough, they will succeed - this realization cannot be erased regardless of how the future unfolds.

When I was directing the after school program for a middle school in Palm Beach County, Florida, I was witness to a challenge that brought out the very best and the most creativity in my students. We were building a giant slingshot to catapult pumpkins across the soccer field. The idea was that we would use the "data" we gathered from each event to learn algebraic equations and we would be using pumpkin' chunkin' data. The kids thought it was magnificently fun, even if it did have to do with algebra. For example, we would measure the weight of the pumpkin and the distance it traveled, and we also mapped the X and Y coordinates of the trajectory using an app for iPads called Vector. Using this tool we were also able to capture the height, speed and parabolic curve of the pumpkin projectile as it arced across the field. The only thing bigger than the pumpkins on the field were the students smiles.

As we were building the slingshot, which was eight feet tall and made of 4X4 pieces of lumber, the students learned all types of skills and they mastered them all; however, one crucial element of the slingshot eluded us and try as we might, we could not solve the "bands problem." It became our biggest challenge for our pumpkin slingshot project.

We were using 6 medical strength rubber tubes on each side of the slingshot, and each tube was 8 feet long. These were tied to the top arms at the top of the slingshot, and the other ends were tied to a burlap sack which had been retired from its former job of transporting coffee beans from Guatemala to a coffee shop in south Florida. The pumpkin would sit in the hammock created by the burlap sack and the students would pull back, stretching the bands thereby storing their collective energy into the bands, and then ka-fwapp! They would let go and pumpkins would fly! But (darn the "but"), after each launch, the tubing would be a completely tangled mess, and in some cases, the pumpkin wouldn't fly straight because the tubing became "jammed up" when one side was more entangled than the other.

We tried many different ways to fix the problem. We recruited the math teachers, but they didn't have any idea. The students then recruited the science teachers but to no avail (although they did use the pumpkin data to help the students understand Joules – very cool!). The students then went and cajoled the school's maintenance crew to come take a look, but they too were mystified. This went on for two days, and we were discussing calling the high school to see if some of their upperclassmen friends would come over and take a look which I thought was brilliant because I did not want them to give up. No stone unturned...

Then, as we all stood around the giant slingshot, painted in the school's colors, just kind of staring at it, trying to think of the next solution, a young lady sidled up next to me. She was neatly dressed, and her hair was impeccably done in perfectly straight, long braids. These braids were exceptional: tight to her scalp and tipped in a multicolored array of bands on the ends which draped across her shoulders. She said, "Mr. Wilkins, I think I know what to do." I said, "What? Tell me your idea please!"

With a wide and bright smile, she said, "Let's braid the tubes!"

It was pandemonium as we took the slingshot down and the girls got to work braiding the surgical tubing into tight braids. The girls giggled at being in the limelight and loved every second, but what they loved most was seeing pumpkins flying and fly they did. We lost some length in the tubing, but the net results were spectacular. Hundreds of pumpkin launches later, we had all the data needed for years of algebra.

There is one neat little tidbit of information I think needs mentioning. As the pumpkin launching phenomenon moved through the curriculum in the students' classes, the art department became involved as well with an idea they had. The students took huge syringes and injected the pumpkins with paint and then rolled out gigantic roles of paper in the target area where the pumpkins would land with a catastrophic crunch. As the pumpkins hit the targets, they would explode and the paint inside would splatter all over the paper, making what the students called flying pumpkin art. It was amazingly fun. Especially when you watched the explosions in slow motion because they were using iPads to record these events as well.

When obstacles and challenges such as "tangling tubes on giant slingshots" are overcome, the resulting stamina and tenacity, or grit as it is now referred to, become new facets in the student's character, and the newly experienced grit begins to transform the participant's pattern of daily thinking into one where confidence and belief in one's own abilities and self-worth allow them the luxury of trying new things, attempting new endeavors and feeling safe in the knowledge they probably have what it takes to see it through. There is safety in knowing that life does, after all, give one multiple opportunities to get it right. Who knew the "do over" was so readily available in the universe!

So, embrace the challenge before you. It may be exactly what you need to grow, to emerge into a more successful, positive and capable you. It is interesting to note that when great sports figures are interviewed about their success, many of them speak to their rise in skill, talent and drive as happening in direct proportion to the skill and drive of their opponents. Without the contender, the champion has no one to challenge them to be better, drive harder and become greater.

The mental, psychological and perhaps spiritual aspect to engaging with and overcoming a challenge is multi-faceted; however, as a teacher I witnessed something with my students I call authentic confidence. I would constantly challenge my students with reading and writing and was always gently pushing them to dig deeper, focus more and just generally, try harder.

Invariably, their efforts would eventually pay off because we all have the ability to grow and succeed. I would witness as my students then began to tackle longer and more difficult tasks *without* my coaching and prompting. As their skills developed, so did their confidence and so did their belief in themselves that they could work and thrive independent of my coaching and supervision. Their confidence was based on real life experience and effort, and it was real. *It was authentic, and they owned it from that point on.*

In summary, challenges are the whet stones of life on which we sharpen our intellect and polish our character.

Chapter Seventeen

The Sea

*If you do not have a plan, if you do not know where you are
headed... you will very likely end up stranded.*
— Author

The sea, the water, calls to me, and ironically, I live in the mountains
by the smoothstoned side of a river where the gentle shoosh, shoosh,
shoosh of the river unceasingly fills the air. Much like the waves on a
beach with their constant caressing of the shore, sometimes soft and
other times with furious shiatsu massage intensity sure to unwind even
the tightest knots in the shoulders of the beach, the sea calls to me.
She reminds me that she is waiting to take me places where I can find
fulfillment, gratitude and satisfaction.

Whether she wears a smooth and silky surface gown of sparkling
emeralds or a gossamer wrap of the deepest blue aquamarine crystals

gently rolling across undulating and rolling curves, her beauty is uncontested and exquisite. And then there is the clear dark of night when the cloak of black diamonds descend upon her and the stars and moon are reflected back so the starlight and moonlight fill both below and above the line of the horizon. Up and down lose meaning as the entire vista is one of shimmering and pulsing points of light that extend into infinity. The sea calls to me and, perhaps, it calls to you too.

The beauty of the sea is magical to say the least, but one of the greatest allures for me has been the attachment of adventure to the sea and the waters that feed her. From scuba diving and spearfishing to charting and plotting a course and traveling from one island to another, the adventure is all encompassing. To be on the sea is to be fully in the present because all of your faculties are called into action and are needed to remain in control of the vessel to reach your destination safely. And to be fully present, completely immersed in the experience is what I consider a vacation for the mind. A vacation from worry and anxiety which live in the future, and a vacation from regret and remorse which live in the past. To live in the present is to exist at that moment with a clean slate.

The water is probably the greatest teacher I have ever known, and as I ponder my circuitous route to becoming a captain I can specifically and unequivocally point to my experiences above and below her surfaces that led me to the point where I had both the knowledge and the confidence to set sail on her. The most amazing thing is that this knowledge and confidence is transferable to all areas of life. For example, to move a vessel from Island A to Island B takes planning: food, water, fuel, weather, currents. There are no gas stations in the middle of the ocean, and you are fairly self reliant, so all systems must be checked and checked again: electric, engines, lines, radar, GPS, navigation (paper and electronic), safety equipment, plumbing (very important - plumbing!). It is interesting that self reliance is not inherited - it is learned over time and honed with experience. It is also time intensive and one needs to be committed to the task of preparation if one wants to be successful.

I had alluded to how transferrable the lessons are from captaining on the sea to captaining in your own daily life. Perhaps, the greatest of all lessons I have learned on the sea is the art and skill of planning. There is exactly zero doubt that if you do not plan your course and your preparations to travel from Island A to Island B, you will not arrive. And worse, you may drift around the ocean desert aimlessly and never reach your destination. You may end up somewhere you never wanted to get to at all like a giant pile of sharp and jagged rocks that can rip the entire bottom out of your vessel and leave you vulnerable, without options and stranded. The same can be said for life: if you do not have a plan, if you do not know where you are headed... you will very likely end up stranded.

The sea, calm and beautiful though she may be, can also be ferocious, unrelenting and terrifying in her fury when the dark gray clouds of her wrath envelope the skies and her waves, like the teeth of a black and gnashing dragon, are higher than the highest point on the vessel. Right there, in that moment, with your stomach in your throat and your legs aching from trying to keep your balance, another lesson is taught, as once again fully in the present, all of your senses, knowledge and confidence are fully called upon to confront and overcome the crisis. You do what must be done. You stand where you must stand, and you do what you must to do to successfully navigate through the storm to safety. These lessons and more transfer over into daily life, and the fact there can be success under those harsh conditions allow one the hope that there can also be success in life. To do this, you must learn to trust yourself.

When it comes to trusting yourself, and really believing in your abilities, there is no substitute for real life, real adventure and real fear that you have to face and work through. What follows is one such experience I recently undertook in the year 2021, back when I used to think I was a brave person. A brave man. Now, I know there are times and there are things that make me tremble...

We piloted *Stay The Course*, our condo on the water, from Ft. Myers to Chattanooga in February 2021, and it was an exciting and fierce adventure with unexpected beauty and unexpected happenings from time to time.

One of those happenings occurred on February 4 as we were navigating up the Tombigbee Waterway. It was a cold day and the waters were running unusually fast. In fact, one of the vessels that had departed a few days before we had texted us to let us know there had been some severe flooding and the river was running about 2 knots faster than usual. This fact, of course, has several implications which must be factored into the navigation: reduced speed, potentially greater fuel consumption, fewer anchorages and finally, the potential for daylight to fade before you need it to because you are running slower.

Additionally, they let us know the river was full of debris, and the flooding had lifted trees off of the banks; now these same trees were floating down the river at a good clip due to the current, and they had been playing tree dodge for two days since leaving Mobile. But, as with most dodgeball style games, it's just a matter of time...

Their prop hit a submerged tree. They never saw the tree (or whatever it was). They never heard it either. They suddenly felt the boat lurch backward, and then a vibration could be felt throughout the entire boat whenever they went to throttle up past 900/1000 rpm. The captain immediately knew what had happened. They limped into Demopolis, Alabama, and had the boat pulled. Sure enough, their prop showed all the telltale signs of having run afoul of some species of large timber or another. With the river the color of chocolate milk, there truly was nothing they could have done to prevent the event, except maybe to have not been traveling up the river to begin with. The things we do to get home...

So, we topped off the tanks in Mobile and with some significant angst and trepidation, and our eyes peeled for flotsam, we headed up the river after leaving Turner Marina on the north end of Mobile Bay and Dogfish River. It was cloudy, cold and the wind was snappy sending us running up to the flybridge or the saloon anytime we stepped outdoors. After all, it was February in Alabama. Chilly describes it, but at the same time does not capture the feeling since the wind kept pushing the chilly air down our windbreakers whenever and wherever she could find even the slightest opening that led to bare skin.

We were moving along at a good clip because we knew we had to put some miles behind us, and the next fueling station was not for 200 miles or so at Bobby's Fish Camp. We were moving at about 20 miles per hour, so we were making good headway, but we kept having to slow down for the tugs with their barges and indeed, we also become engaged in a huge game of "now you see 'em, now you don't" with all types of debris and trees that were floating down the river. It simply was not safe to go that fast. We also noticed our gas gauges were plummeting since we were fighting the tremendous current which was absolutely going faster than usual. A fact we later confirmed with several other boat captains...

Taking into account our new navigational conditions, we throttled back to 10 miles per hour which allowed for ample reaction and maneuvering time as we tried to guesstimate how far away was that tree coming right toward us. Of course, the most fun was having to thread the needle between a tree so big Paul Bunyan would have been proud of it and the oversized and powerful tug pushing 12 barges directly toward us. All in all, we had about 40 to 50 feet in width to play with as the enormous front wave from the tug surged under our prow. It was a very "uplifting" experience to say the least.

At around 3 pm we started looking at the very few anchorages detailed in the charts for this area, and, by the way, there are very, very few! Originally, we had wanted to get to Old Lock 1 and pull into the lagoon that exists next to the lock, but there was no possible way we were going to make it before nightfall. So, we pressed on and examined each anchorage and to our dismay, each one was stacked up with trees or the current was moving so fast in them there would have been no way to stay there without using our docking lines to tie off to the trees alongside the bank. With the current screaming obscenities at us, there was no way I was going to launch the dinghy from our flybridge and into the water with our crane davit to run the lines over the trees. Just simply, no way.

We kept checking each anchorage, and I just wasn't happy. None of these anchorages were safe, so at around 5 pm-ish (emphasis on the "ish") I threw the boat onto plane and began to hightail it to Old Lock 1. I didn't wan't to play chicken with the river in the dark, but I was going to have to it seemed. At least, with the last daylight available, I would cover as much river as I could. All 39,000 pounds of *Stay The Course* was skimming across the top of the river, and it was our version of flying.

We were one mile from the lock and what we hoped would be a good anchorage when total darkness descended on the river and our little band of four musketeers. The clouds above were thick, so there was no starlight, no moonlight and there were no lights along the river at that point. Total, inky darkness was our new reality except for the dimly lit electronics on the flybridge and the spotlight on the pulpit railing of the bow. We also had one 50,000 lumens handheld spotlight which we used to pan the river a hundred yards or so ahead of the boat. I have discovered the standard spotlight on the pulpit railing doesn't really spot much in conditions of deep darkness. So, my wife, our two friends and I had all eight eyes squinting into the night, up the river, looking for anything that might reflect back from our two spotlights which skimmed across the surface. We did this very, very slowly as *Stay the Course* moved up the river for a painstakingly slow mile.

My eyes darted from the river to the Garmin instruments as I kept the boat on the navigation line. Back and forth my head swiveled, and finally I could tell from the Garmin display that we had pulled up alongside, and were parallel to, the supposed entrance to the channel that goes into the lagoon at the lock. Slowly and carefully we maneuvered the vessel over to where the entrance should be, and the only visible thing were tall grasses with a plentitude of trees behind them. Inch by inch and foot by foot we moved forward until we found a break in the grasses about 20 feet wide. Shining the light over to the trees, we could see they had become spread apart by about 20 feet as well. Our beam is 14'11", and I have learned over time that twenty feet of width is plenty to maneuvre in. We inched our way forward using the handheld beam to check either side of the boat. The depth reading on the Garmin was 5 feet. In my world, having been all over the islands in the Gulf down by Captiva and Sanibel, five feet is pretty roomy. We pushed forward into the little channel toward the trees, the handheld illuminating the trees so they looked like giant timber gargoyles ready to gobble up the *Stay The Course* and us with it.

Quite suddenly, the grasses were gone, and we slowly moved under the canopy of trees that covered the channel and then we saw them. Several trees had fallen into the channel from the sides of the bank, probably the result of the flooding having softened the earth so completely. The channel narrowed, and then we could see the channel made a sharp turn to port. As we approached the trees, I had already made the decision if we ran aground, that would be fine. We were out of the river and the current had subsided. At this very dark moment, I knew we would be relatively safe. I stood at the helm not touching the ship's wheel which I had centered, and the fingers of my left hand lightly, feather light, controlled the throttle controls. Very small moves... My right hand was positioned over the bow thruster, and each small thrust was just a quick touch of the joystick. Nothing more. I kept repeating the mantra in my head over and over, "Slow is pro. Slow is pro. Slow is pro..."

Stay The Course eased forward. I looked down at my hands and saw my fingers were trembling. All communication was done is hushed voices, and my wife proclaimed in a shaky voice, I think trying to break the silence, "It's so dark... I can't see anything..." We were snaking around one of the downed trees and the branches slowly and softly scratched down the side of the boat and my spine tingled. Another downed tree emerged in front of us. I brought the boat to a stop. I thought I could sneak past if I rotated the boat 60 degrees to port without forward or backward movement. I told my friend, standing next to me holding the handheld spotlight, the plan. An experienced boater himself, he nodded his agreement. It was a good plan. We began to rotate the boat. The depth was reading 2 feet. We inched forward. The depth read 1.1 feet. The branches closed in tighter and were touching both sides of the boat. The handheld light momentarily pointed ahead, and we could see the lagoon in full view. Maybe 100 feet or less. We were so close...

I inched forward and the depth increased to 3 feet, and then Charlie, quietly standing next to me, calmly said, "To port six inches." I didn't ask why. I knew he wouldn't have said it if it wasn't necessary.

Deftly, the I moved the boat six inches and watched as another fallen tree slid past the starboard side. We had just missed it, and it was indeed six inches. Then, just like that, we were in the lagoon where the depth read 9 feet, the water was dead calm and the clouds broke apart while starlight began streaming down like fireflies onto the surface of the water.

I looked down, my hands were still shaking.

When I think about my next voyage, my next trip to or on the water, I can barely wait. I am nervously excited, and I assure you, it is one the greatest reasons I get up in the morning and look forward to the future.

Chapter Eighteen

Family

I was blessed with a great family. We support each other in the good times and the bad times, and we rely on each other to hear the unvarnished truth about whatever happens to be the latest drama in our lives. You know, the kind of truths normal friends and acquaintances will not share with you for fear of offending you. Therefore, I count on my family to "tell it like it is," and if that involves some perceived slight or another to my fragile ego, then that is perfectly fine.

In short, we have each other's back as they say in today's vernacular, and that leaves me, to a certain degree, with a feeling of safety. It allows me to go about the business of life knowing that if times get tough, then the tough will get going, and many of those tough folks are in my family's camp.

So then, what comprises a family, or more accurately, who comprise the members of a family?

I don't necessarily believe that families are only biological in nature. In fact, I think nature bears out that family is indeed not only biological since each family is comprised of two independent individuals from different parents making a conscious, and in some cases, unconscious decisions to create a new family. Thus, the children, grandchildren and so on can be biological or they may not be, as with adopted children, foster children and the myriad other combinations we find where children are living with those that care for and nurture them. All one needs to do is think about all of the blended families there are throughout the world to understand this truth. However, with that realization as a foundation, here is where my definition of family begins to expand, deepen and widen. The words care and nurture just mentioned begin to curate a new idea and definition of what a family might be and certainly is for me.

To care, nurture, support and love someone in such a manner that their needs are put first, ahead of your own, or at the very least on par with your own needs and wants, is my evolving definition of a family member.

Examining my own life, my wife and I have two above and beyond friends whom we have been friends with for over thirty years, and we have literally been through thick and thin together. We share our dreams with each other. We travel and vacation together. We chat weekly about all the latest goings-on, and perhaps most importantly, the four of us provide an honest and well-tempered sounding board for each other concerning the dramas that constantly are unfolding in our lives. I find it so vitally important to have people you can reach out to you know will provide feedback that is raw and unvarnished. Truth matters and real friends and family will deliver it.

Good life decisions can only be made with good and honest feedback from the, usually, very small circle of friends and family whom we trust completely. They can be the veritable lifeline we hear about so often. It has been many years now that we stopped referring to ourselves as friends. The four of us have been family for years, and even to this day I call them "brother" and "sister."

Harkening back to the terms care, nurture and support, sometimes we have members of our family that are none of these where we are concerned. In fact, I know of several instances where a family member, unfortunately, showed a lack of support, lack of caring and more disturbingly was actually destructive to one or more members of their family.

When we are subjected to destructive individuals, family or not, we have a responsibility to ourselves to safeguard against them. We have to be our own greatest heroes in this regard. You must be there for yourself. Protect and love yourself first that you may protect and love someone else later when needed.

There is a spectrum where negative and destructive people are involved in your life. Physical and emotional violence are, perhaps, one end of the spectrum while petty lies and gossip might be the other. Each incidence deserves a response that is calibrated and effective to the occurred offense. So, physical violence requires law enforcement intervention closely followed by a restraining and distancing order. Petty lies and gossip require the face-to-face conversation to set the record straight and let the person know the boundaries of what will and what will not be tolerated by you. None of us are perfect, and sure as the sun sets and rises, our feathers will get ruffled from time to time, so it's important to distinguish between a moment of disquiet and torpitude versus truly destructive behavior.

Unfortunately, my own family has extensive experience in this arena as one of the biological parents of our four children became, and still is, psychologically abusive. The abuse started when they were very young, and it continues to this day even though my children are in their thirties. In many cases, the abuse also became physical, and the effects of this abuse became lifelong afflictions that required counseling, discovery and probing at the very deepest levels of their psyche. These types of traumas affected our children deeply and affect the way they manage their own relationships, interact with their children and very importantly as well, how they view the world around them.

It is hard to see the world as a good place when you have repeatedly been told in words and actions how worthless you are. Nothing is quite so damaging to a 5, 8 and 10 year old. Actually, the damage is incalculable at any age.

My wife and I would literally be sick with fear and grief every time a weekend rolled around where the children needed to spend time with our exs, but the children never knew this as we knew they needed to be free mentally and not feel guilt when they were apart from us. We packed them up and sent them off with big smiles and lots of waving goodbye. We knew creating a blended family would be hard, but we had no idea of the jealousy, vitriol and cruelty that would be wielded by our ex partners. They almost made it impossible; yet, love prevailed.

Each of our children, of their own accord and without our input, have severed ties with their other biological parent. They did this to safeguard their mental health and, in one instance, to safeguard their physical health. I am not certain, but I also believe this was done to safeguard the mental health of their own children as they could not trust what would be said or done in front of their own children, our grandchildren. Sometimes difficult and painful decisions need to be made about who will and who will not be included in our family, but these decisions can make all the difference between positive, loving outcomes and negative, destructive outcomes.

Protect your family. Protect yourself.

So, a beautiful family, with all of the members you decide to incorporate into your family matrix, is a wonderful community to belong to. It adds context, color and love in our world, and to belong, to truly know you are a part of something where you can give back as much as you receive, is an incredibly rich and gratifying experience.

I get up each and every day and sit in my rocking chair sharing a cup of coffee with my best friend, looking out of our bedroom window at the promise of a new day, and I always ask with a smile on my face, "I wonder what everyone is doing today?"

Chapter Nineteen

God

I close my eyes and the soothing velvet of darkness envelopes my mind, so that I can clearly see that from night follows day, from darkness follows light and from God follows Man. Further, from God follows Me.

— Author

The realization came in an instant. We are one.

Writing about the All That Is, the Universe, or as so many, including myself, would characterize it, God, has given me pause. I have been here, stuck in the pause mode for four months. Oh sure, I started out by whiteboarding the entire chapter, and the board filled up quickly. I ran out of room, and I decided I was making something simple and beautiful into something chaotic and complicated. I was overreaching with concepts, theories and assumptions, and the arrogance of such a vain act did not escape me.

After all, who am I to speak of God? Who am I to believe that what I have to say matters in regard to the maker and shaper of all that is? These questions made me feel small but not insignificant. I am small, but I matter. After all, it takes many drops of water to make an ocean, and each drop of water is necessary for the ocean to exist.

It is fair to ask ourselves hard questions, and it is also fair to occasionally shake the foundations of our lives and our beliefs with these same questions. Not only is it fair, but I believe it can only serve our best interests and those of all we come into contact with - to be introspective and reflective about our motives and actions. What do we really believe? Are they our beliefs or someone else's beliefs gradually foisted upon us over time with the kindest and most loving of intentions? A lifetime of accidental or very purposeful indoctrination? Or a lifetime of true faith? Perhaps, both at the same time? It's fair to ask these questions because only then can we know if we truly believe of our own accord versus simply just following the herd of spiritual safety.

I think these past four months have been just that. A series of questions that needed answers and a lot of thinking and meditation. As I sit here in my comfy office chair (and thank goodness for the wonderful butthugging office chair), I can look back and see that even though I was on "pause," the wheels were still spinning in the furthest recesses of my subconscious. Thinking about big things, it would appear, takes big time.

The last four months my thoughts continually hearkened back to the whiteboard, the topic of God - the all consuming reality that we exist within his? hers? its?, body. We exist because we have been allowed to exist. That last phrase is startling in its far-reaching implications: something or someone (God?) allows us to exist. How profound a realization is that, and by default, gratitude pours from me like a thousand waterfalls all loudly thanking the All That Is for allowing this small droplet of water to be a part of the ebb and flow of the ocean. The ebb and flow of the universe.

As the rusty wheels churned inside my head, my subconscious wrestled with the two opposing ideas of the spiritual coin: I am nothing and no one to speak about God as I am but one lowly man who is not specifically versed in one doctrine or another versus I am a product of the universe God created and as such, by divine right, a child of God. Perhaps, even, I am a spark of God as a member of the fabric of the universe. Am I a single and short strand in the tapestry of the cosmos? Perhaps. Just perhaps.

After some serious meditation, I think both possibilities can be true at the same time. The paradox of the spiritual dilemma is that we are only a spark of the All That Is, but we are a spark nonetheless. Therefore, we can speak to the part that is ours and to the connection we each have to God. Regardless of how small that direct connection is or not. However, we may not be privy to and/or have a full understanding of the "Big Picture." Our minds, our understandings are still young. I think we can all agree that as individuals, and as a species, we have much to learn. And, more to the point, more collective wisdom to acquire as the millenia are experienced. As regards the universe, we are neophytes.

I am an intuitive being, and I always have been. Somehow, someway, I knew I was connected in some deep cellular and spiritual way to something much greater than myself. This is also a source of great comfort as well. It is inexplicable but at the same time completely reasonable. It is akin to moving down the highway in a car at 70 miles per hour; the body does not feel it is moving forward - yet we are, and we know it.

So it is with our lifelong ride-a-long with God. We are riding along the entire time, but we just don't "feel it." Until we do, and then, we are suddenly awake and keenly aware of our connectivity with the bigger program, and this happened to me when I was a young boy.

When I was ten, circa 1974, my father became very ill. This very large 6'3" man shrunk in size to a skeletal 163 pounds as he lay in a bed in the very prestigious Duke hospital in Durham, North Carolina. His team of doctors could not determine what type of intestinal ailment he was suffering from, and day after day he continued to waste away, vanishing before our eyes. The x-ray showed his small intestine had shriveled in circumference and was badly damaged and disfigured as if some wild animal were chewing on it. To everyone's dismay, the doctors announced they would need to remove the intestine and attach a colostomy bag to his side. My father was depressed, spent and on the verge of giving up. Mostly, he was just tired.

On the day before the surgery, my father spoke to my mother and said he needed to tell her a few things should he not make it which he felt was very real possibility. Knowing the pragmatic nature of my father, ever the provider and a good one at that, I imagine they went over finances, the will and finally, at the end, how much he loved her. My father, pragmatic though he was, had an enormous romantic streak running right down the middle of his large back as evidenced by his vinyl record collection which included the smooth saxophone of Boots Randolph and the strong, melodious sounds of the famous Mexican vocalist Pedro Vargas. These were the sounds I grew up with every Sunday morning as we all padded around the house nibbling on breakfast in our slippers. An international man of intrigue born in rural North Carolina.

The following morning was the surgery and the angst in the house was palpable. My mother was a nervous wreck. I was ten and really didn't fully understand the implications of the surgery, but I was still in shock at seeing my father in the condition he was in. I wasn't immune to my mother's red-rimmed eyes although I really didn't know what to do about it. What could I, a boy of 10, really do about anything that mattered? I firmly believed the answer was nothing. The night before the surgery, as we settled in for a long night, I had a dream.

Jesus came to me in the middle of the night. I could not see his face, but I could see his body and his hands, and I recognized the open wounds in the center of his palms when he took my hands in his. His light brown hands were calloused and rough. Almost dusty. His robes, hanging in big folds from his forearms, were a course tweed fabric that were long and hung down almost to his brown feet which were clad in leather sandals. His skin had a glow to it, and it appeared that light emanated from him. The dream seemed completely real to me, and to this day I can recall every single moment and word of this dream. It is a complete memory of something that did happen to me, and I also remember at no point did I feel afraid. In fact, I felt love. Just love.

Jesus took my hands in his, placed a golden coin in my hand, and he instructed me, "Go take this golden coin to your mother. Tell her that everything will be fine and give her this golden coin. Go now." The instant he said, "Go now," I woke completely up. No morning fogginess and no needing a moment to fully wake up – I was absolutely clear eyed and wide awake. I felt more alert, clear than I had ever felt in my life. My hand was clinched tightly where I held the golden coin, and I ran into my mother's room excitedly telling her that Jesus had come to me and given me a golden coin and Dad was going to be okay!

My mom patiently had me tell her the entire dream. My hand still clinched, I opened it and was confused to find no coin, but my mother said, "That's okay. It's a dream coin, and you've already given it to me. Thank you." I suppose where Jesus is concerned, gold isn't the only currency that has value.

Years later, my mom told me the instant I told her what Jesus had said, her worries instantly vanished. She knew it to be "truth." Later that morning she received a call from the hospital. The surgery had been canceled, and they knew what was wrong with Dad, and it was completely curable with antibiotics! At the time this happened we lived in Costa Rica, and he had contracted amoebas, probably from drinking the local water, which at that time did not have the same health and cleanliness safeguards we do today. Amoebas are not something seen very often in the US, and so, even though the doctors had ordered a lab test for them as a long shot, they had not received the results yet and needed to move forward with the surgery to save his life – until that morning.

You see, a lab tech cleaning in the laboratory where they receive test results found my father's results for the test where they had fallen behind a shelve. It was positive for amoebas... So, no surgery would be required. God does work in mysterious ways, and sometimes it involves, well let's just say, a little cleaning and a little gold to boot.

In my experience, the connection with God is individual for each of us, yet universal in nature. At the end of the day it is this experience, directly with God, just because you exist, that can bring profound and peace if we can truly believe we are worthy of love, and we are. I have this relationship with God and so do you.

So, then, we are here having our experience of this lifetime because God created this existence, and we are also a part of the actual fabric God created for this universe. How does that make you feel? Special?

It should! How absolutely freeing and wonderful to understand that I, we, you are not alone and you are part of something so incredible, magnificent and ultimately, beautiful: life.

You are connected to every other person, thing, place and idea that comprises the everything that is. After all, it is all God. God is not without. God is the outside, the inside and the space that holds both at the same time. And you, my beautiful friend, are a spark, one of the lights, of the All That Is.

Remember those four months where I had my hiatus from writing this chapter? I became very ill during that time, and I am thankful now it happened (easy to say once recovered right?) because it changed my paradigm. It shifted my thought pattern to a simpler and kinder way of looking at the world. I went from 240 lbs to 200 lbs very quickly, and I could not walk for several days as a horrible infection invaded my spinal canal and hips. I was humbled to my knees by a force I could not see.

I used to wake up and spring out of bed, ready to take on the world; now, the first thing I do is give thanks that I have another day. I am thankful to have woken up feeling healthy, not in pain, and yes, alive. Every morning I sit and have coffee with my best friend and I give thanks. I am grateful for the time we have. I am keenly, acutely dialed in, connected in a deeply satisfying, and personal level, to God.

I am fortunate to still be able to play my part in the universe God created. Every morning I invest a prayer and give thanks that I am a spark of God and am aware of the divine relationship between us. God, you, and me: we are all one, and every day is a great reason to be alive to experience that peace and belief.

Chapter Twenty

Children

What I find to be the most vital aspect to having raised four fully independent human beings has been the ability, and difficulty, with instilling within them the belief that they are enough.

— Author

When my daughter was born, I felt a shift in the universe. At first it was a small tremor, almost like the small tremors of excitement we have from time to time as children when we know with certainty that something wonderful and magical is about to happen.

Born through a cesarean section, and slightly jaundiced after a twenty-three and a half hour hard labor, she was whisked away to the neonatal unit to be put under the lights, and the complete irony was that, from my perspective, it was her light in the room that brightly illuminated every nook, cranny and eye in the room. There was nothing or no one brighter than her at that moment.

Then I held her. Time came to a halt, and the world roared loudly in my ears as the cloak of parental responsibility settled onto my shoulders with a thunderclap. I understood that everything I thought had ever mattered, did not matter at all. What really mattered, what truly needed to be the center of the universe, was safely cradled in my arms, Dad's arms, and very fast asleep. I will never forget that moment for as long as I live. Fatherhood was an awakening to something much greater than myself, and to behold my child for the first time was completely and utterly breathtaking. I was very smitten and very in love.

Life, with its ups, downs, ins and outs, moved along as it always does, and some years later as I stepped up to the plate to take a swing, life threw me a fast curve ball. I found myself the stepfather for three more children whose gradual but sudden appearance in my life expanded the definition of what I thought a father was, or at least, ought, to be. It was like having an instant family. Pour in the life juice, add the contents of the Big Ole' Family package and stir furiously and voila, here we were, the six of us!

These four children, biological and through marriage to my wife, were to become the center of my universe for the next 18 or so years, and they remain part of my daily interactions to this day. Most every thought, financial strategy, activity and idea has the kids' well-being as part of the backdrop in my decision-making tree. Consequently, there are very few big decisions that don't have me trying to align our, meaning my wife and I, and their, meaning the four musketeers, best interests simultaneously. As with most "big" decisions in life, they are sometimes made up over time by the total sum of all the small decisions we make on a daily basis. Many have been the time when

I made a decision subconsciously (or it is it unconsciously?), and I didn't know it had happened until afterward. Then, as I reflected back on my actions, I could plainly see that all of the smaller decisions had led to their inevitable conclusion.

It is not only about leaving a legacy, which is an important ideal if it can be achieved, but what I find to be the most vital aspect to having raised four fully independent human beings has been the ability, and difficulty, with instilling within them the belief that they are enough. They have everything needed to go out into the world and become who they really are. They all know how to become the best version of themselves possible, and if they aren't sure, they certainly know enough to ask the right questions. *In short, Karla and I decided long ago the best children we could raise would be the children that needed us the least.*

From school to sports, checkers, scuba diving, listening to Tolkien on long car rides and movie nights every other Sunday when they returned home from their other parents, the children taught me that we are here to do for others. As I have moved into my fifties and sixties, this idea, that we are here to do for others, has grown bigger in its scope. *Our community, our tribe, grows larger over the years, and it becomes much more apparent that we belong to, and are an important part of, something much greater than ourselves.*

We may feel like the center of the universe, but this illusion is brought about by our biological experience which, as we all know over time, is restricted and limited by our physical existence. We are more, much more to the those we love and care for than the physical boundaries of our bodies.

My four beautiful children have brought me several lifetimes of joy, and their ups and downs have become mine. Of course, I, we, cannot be the solutions to their problems just as we cannot be the source of their successes. They must continue to accomplish success and tackle problems on their own so they may have the real and authentic confidence these experiences imbue. Confidence and belief in themselves are theirs to call upon when they are most sorely needed.

Without a doubt, I cannot imagine my life without my children in it. I find the love I hold for them incalculable, and if ever I am challenged with depressing thoughts and feelings, all I have to do is think about them for just a moment and the world feels better. They are, indeed, one of my favorite reasons to be alive.

Chapter Twenty-One

To Be Yourself

Wouldn't it be positively and absolutely exquisite to feel and experience the true and authentic you?
— Author

So, here you are. Just you and another day before you full of potential, full of promise or just as possible, full of trepidation, full of doom, anger, sadness, fear...

Albeit, whether your day is full of promise or full of pitfalls matters not one iota does it? In the most simple of metaphors, and in this case the metaphor fits like a glove, life with all of its ups and downs is simply the great competition. Life is moving the ball up and down the field and up and down the court. Life is moving the chess pieces on the board regardless of whether you're black or white on any given day. Life is participating in the field, arena, stadium, court and course and here is the thing, there are only four roles you can play: you can be in the competition, you can be a spectator and watch the competition, you can be coordinator and administrator for the competition or you can be completely disinterested and have nothing to do with the competition. Those are the four options and by default, you will fill one of these roles.

Which role you choose is totally up to you, and this is so vitally important. The one you choose is perfectly okay and wonderful... as long as you perform the role to the best of your ability.

This is the key to enjoying every single moment and knowing it was worthwhile. Each role is different and important. No one role is better than another, and each role is important in making the other three roles matter in their own right.

Let's examine this idea by looking at a soccer game during the World Cup. The players will compete against each other representing their countries and their citizenry. The fans will fill the stadium and are the actual reason the players are there. The players are there representing their fans. The organizers ensure the match has rules and regulations and will provide the much needed integrity which all contenders need in a competition that is worthy. Everyone else not in attendance makes everyone in attendance feel very special they are there! Ironic, I know.

As I have probably mentioned many times before, I have four wonderful children that are now well into adulthood, but there was a time not that long ago when they were itty bitty rug rats running amuck in the house and the neighborhood as they played every sport imaginable; however, it was roller hockey and ice hockey that finally became the one sport they could all play together. They all became experts at slamming pucks while skating at full speed and simultaneously ensuring they got a few good licks in while they sped past their friends on the opposing team. Helmets, heavy padding and a healthy dose of competitive sportsmanship ensured that injuries were a rarity, and afterward, as we all ate at one pizza joint or another, they would good naturedly rib each other about this particular jab, poke or push that had sent one or the other skimming across the frozen rink. Laughter and togetherness were the common themes at these events.

I vividly recall sitting in the stands hour after hour, weekend after weekend for many of these games when our son or daughter would look up into the stands, scanning the faces. Searching. When our eyes finally locked, an enormous smile would spread across their face and they would raise their hockey stick in salute. We waved, gigantic proud parent smiles stickered across our faces, and then we ended the connection by hooting and hollering our support.

Our role, to spectate and be in the stands and not in the game but instead in complete support of it and our children players, was one of the greatest experiences in my life. I often hear the phrase that goes something like, "If you not on the court, then you're not in the game of life." That is a very shallow and narrow view of the world, and it negates the importance of each role to be played. I assure you for our children, it was very important we were their biggest fans in the stands as they took center ice.

Each role is important. Important for each individual fulfilling the role, and in turn, each person benefits from each of the other participants fulfilling their roles.

So, venture forth with courage and resolution. Choose the role that calls to you and perform it to the very best of your ability. You are here now, so why not give it a go? Why not offer life the opportunity to bring you satisfaction? Wouldn't it be positively and absolutely exquisite to feel and experience the true and authentic you? To live in a way you know honors who you really are?

As I write this, it has dawned on me that what I am describing could be considered living free. Completely free to choose the role you want to fill right now, and that is an honest and true reason to live.

About The Author

Chris is an educator, writer, photographer, adventurer and serial entrepreneur. When he is not writing, you will find him taking pictures of something unusual or interesting that has piqued his curiosity. It is this constant state of inquiry that drives Chris to search for understanding and beauty in the world we live in. If anything, he hopes to leave the world just a bit better than he found it and to share its magnificence and beauty with you.

Chapter Twenty-Two

Books By This Author

Thoughts Provoked

Thoughts Provoked is a collection of poems and short stories that are both old and new as they relate to the author's life. A collection of moments memorialized on the page lest they are forgotten in the rapidly approaching winter of life, old age.

Through Life's Keyhole

This collection of poems is not for the feint of heart, so tread carefully lest long dormant emotions suddenly come to life in your dreams and waking moments alike. Life spins her loom around us, in us and through us, and these poems capture the threads as they swirl past to weave moments in time.

Mountain Musings... An Unusual Conversation

Mountain Musings... An Unusual Conversation is a collection of photographs and narrative reflections about the Appalachian Mountains of North Georgia and the people who live in them.

Project Based Learning for Out of School Time

Project Based Learning has proven to be one of the most successful strategies for student learning; however, this learning isn't only academic. It also encompasses the 21st century skills which are so important now that we have fully moved away from an industrial age. This book is a primer for anyone seeking to implement PBL strategies, methodologies and lesson plans in their after school program.